CATHOLIC EVANGELIZATION

Catholic Evangelization

Stories of Conversion and Witness

Edited by Steve Dawson

IGNATIUS PRESS SAN FRANCISCO

Originally published as
Catholic Street Evangelization
in 2016

Cover by Enrique J. Aguilar

St. Paul Street Evangelization logo
by the Alice Paul Group

ISBN: 978-1-62164-664-8 (PB)
ISBN 978-1-64229-291-6 (eBook)
Library of Congress Control Number 2014949939
Printed in the United States of America ♾

Editor's Dedication

To the Sacred Heart of Jesus;
Our Lady of Guadalupe, Star of the New Evangelization;
my wife, Maria; my children, Maximilian and Maris;
and all the evangelists of St. Paul Street Evangelization

CONTENTS

FOREWORD

The Bible talks a lot about feet. Do a biblical search and you will find the words *feet* or *foot* mentioned over 380 times—the "washing of feet" is found at least seventeen times. The most well-known instance, of course, is Jesus washing the feet of His disciples.

It is not surprising that foot washing was so ubiquitous in biblical times. Travel was mainly by foot on dusty paths or muddy trails where camels, donkeys, and other animals made a mess everywhere. People either went barefoot or wore simple sandals that offered little protection from the grime of the ground. Feet were considered filthy; they were in constant contact with the earth and a symbol of man's contamination by contact with the sinful world.

In the Middle East today, feet are still considered dirty. One Sunday while sitting at Mass in Bethlehem, I innocently crossed my legs. Suddenly, a man seated near me jumped up and whacked my leg, knocking my foot to the floor. That was my lesson that it is considered rude to expose the bottom of one's feet in a church in the Middle East.

In such a culture it would be hard to imagine anyone saying that feet are beautiful. But that is exactly what the Prophet Isaiah says: "How beautiful upon the mountains are the feet of him who brings good tidings" (Is 52:7). The herald runs along the mountain ridges, proclaiming his message to all who will listen. His feet carry him along, and the recipients thank God for his beautiful feet, the feet that spread the good news.

Saint Paul applied Isaiah's "beautiful feet" to preaching the gospel of Jesus Christ. To the Romans he wrote, "For, 'every one who calls upon the name of the Lord will be saved.' But how are men to call upon him in whom they have not believed? And how are they to believe in him of whom they have never heard? And how are they to hear without a preacher? And how can men preach unless they are sent? As it is written, 'How beautiful are the feet of those who preach good news!'" (Rom 10:13–15).

And such good news! It is news of a loving God's real existence, salvation from sin in a world gone mad, the resurrection of the dead, and the life of the world to come. It is marvelous news, but it doesn't reach anyone's ears until a messenger with beautiful feet shouts it from the mountaintops—and the town squares of cities everywhere.

But who is called to deliver this good news? The priest, pastor, or religious? The trained orator, public speaker, or radio host? Yes, all of them, but also everyone who has been baptized in the Name of the Father, the Son, and the Holy Spirit. By virtue of our baptism we have all been appointed evangelists—people with feet and tongues to take the gospel of Jesus Christ to a very needy world.

The Church has told us from the beginning that we're all called to share the message of Jesus Christ. The *Catechism* says, "Baptism, Confirmation, and Eucharist are sacraments of Christian initiation. They ground the common vocation of all Christ's disciples, a vocation to holiness and to the mission of evangelizing the world" (*CCC* 1533). It is our mission, our individual responsibility, and we will be held accountable on the Last Day for how well we fulfilled God's requirements.

But wait a minute. We are Catholics, not Bible-thumping Evangelical Protestants. We don't do evangelizing and sharing our faith with other people, right?

Whenever I tell my conversion story, my dad holds a prominent place. In 1953 he reached a crisis in his life and cried out to God, "I don't know if you even exist, but if you do, please reveal yourself to me—I am desperate!" At work the next morning his prayer was answered. A man approached my dad out of the blue saying, "Charlie Ray, you need Jesus Christ in your life." My dad was shocked the answer had come so soon. What beautiful words—the man told him of God's love, salvation, and eternal life. And my dad believed.

I always ask my audience, "Do you think it was a Catholic who spoke to my dad about Jesus?" I always get the same response—heads shaking, a few chuckles, and many who say no. Isn't that a shame? It is our gospel. The Bible is a Catholic book. We as Catholics have a history of taking the gospel of Christ to the farthest reaches of the world, but in recent times we have become silent. The common response is, "My faith is private; my religion is personal. It is not something we *talk* about!"

Our whole family is glad the Baptist gentleman approached my dad that morning in 1953 because it has transformed us. The man believed it was his responsibility to tell people the saving message of Jesus Christ. This message, truncated though it was as presented by a Baptist, had a profound impact. Now the second, third, and fourth generations have taken it a step further and discovered the fullness of the Christian faith in the heart of the Catholic Church.

Evangelization is the art of sharing what is important to us. If we win a million dollars, do we keep it to ourselves? If we find a miracle cure for a disease, do we fail to share it with family and friends? Why, then, when we discover and believe in the eternal and loving God who has opened the door to eternal life and bliss forever, do we not share that news with others?

St. Paul Street Evangelization is again putting into practice what Christians in past centuries did with joy and vigor. Had early Christians not brought the gospel to new lands and peoples, we would all be pagans today, lost in our sins, without God and without hope in the world. Someone was called, someone was sent, someone had beautiful feet to bring the news of salvation and eternal life to us. Someone broke loose from his comfort zone and did the right thing.

Steve Dawson and his team of modern-day "apostles" have undertaken the momentous task of teaching Catholics to step up and live out their calling. They are again taking Jesus Christ to the pagans—those on the streets of America and the world. Many people are being re-evangelized. Many Catholics are being trained and encouraged, and are going out as a new army of preachers. But the preaching is not "in your face"; rather, it is a beautiful message shared on the streets with a smile, an encouraging word, a Rosary, and a bold expression of love and gentleness as the truth is proclaimed.

Thanks to Steve Dawson and all those who work with him; all the bishops, priests, deacons, and religious who support and join them; and all the lay people from every walk of life—all awakening to the excitement, joy, and thrill of living out their call as evangelists. How beautiful are the feet and the words of those who bring good news!

Saint Paul, great evangelist and example, pray for us! Amen.

Steve Ray

INTRODUCTION

By accident, my wife left a jar open on the kitchen counter all night. It contained about a quarter inch of honey. In the morning she found, mired at the bottom, six ants who had ventured their way to a sweet and sticky death.

The jar reminded me of our home's ant problem and my need to spray the foundation with insecticide. But it also struck me as a powerful image of a much bigger problem than insect infestation.

Like those ants, millions in today's secular culture seek pleasure and material fulfillment to the point of their own demise. The goods and faculties that God created as *good*—possessions, food and drink, sex, health, work, relationships, freedom, art, science—are pursued in such inordinate amounts and in such disordered ways, that they entrap and engulf their pursuers, spiritually swamping them. Honey is good, but not if it surrounds you to the point of drowning.

There was a period in my own life when I was stuck in such a lethal swamp. I was spiritually dead but continued to gorge myself on this world's pleasures. But God rescued me ("His mercy endures forever!"), and as they say, "I lived to tell the tale."

In this book, you'll find my tale. But more importantly, you'll find an account of what God did after He rescued me.

St. Paul Street Evangelization is an organization that God used me to found for the purpose of trying to extract more souls from the swamp. I have come to understand that the reason this deadly spiritual quagmire exists is that people have largely abandoned God. They are left with a faulty moral compass and so devise their own guidelines for the use of this world's goods (e.g., "If it feels right, I do it.") and often end up sucked into the quicksand.

The means of rescue, therefore, lies in bringing God back to His rightful, primary place in people's lives. It involves (re)introducing them to the Person of Jesus Christ and His life-giving plan for their lives within the fold of His Holy Catholic Church.

That's what we do at St. Paul Street Evangelization (SPSE). All over the country and beyond, teams of faithful Catholics go out to public places—a park, a farmers' market, a sports stadium—for the express purpose of telling others about Jesus and His Church.

In this book you'll read their stories. I've highlighted a sampling of SPSE evangelists and the encounters they've had in their own cities or towns—from the folks in Boise who are at the park every Sunday from 2:00 to 3:00 P.M., to the team on the Strip in Las Vegas, to Uzi in Chicago's gang territory. I am confident that the Holy Spirit is at work in every street-evangelization outing, whether any fruit is apparent or not, but I am awed and humbled when He gives us the gift of an evident change of heart or spiritual realization in someone who has just heard the gospel message.

When I've just met someone who is a strong Catholic with an active faith life, I have the propensity to ask him, "Have you always been a faithful Catholic?" I imagine I'm not alone in that tendency. So, I've anticipated your question, "Have they always been faithful Catholics?" by providing the evangelists' own conversion stories as well. Many of our evangelists themselves were delivered from the muck of the amoral swamp, and, like mine, their rescues have helped fuel their drive to embrace and spread the gospel of Jesus Christ.

But there is a better reason for including the evangelists' own stories. Sharing the way God has worked in one's life personally is key to making the Christian message tangible and real to those who hear it. It is key to evangelization. If the essence of being a Christian is to have a living, intimate relationship with Jesus, then it only makes sense for evangelists to tell others about that relationship! Indeed, the evangelist par excellence, Saint Paul, gives his conversion story twice in the Acts of the Apostles (in chapters 22 and 26, in addition to Saint Luke's account in chapter 9) and then again in his Letter to the Galatians (in chapter 1). To emphasize the importance of the personal testimony in spreading the gospel, I have included our evangelists' own conversion stories in this book. They are another link in the chain of passing on the faith.

My goal in sharing these stories from the street and the evangelists' personal testimonies is to show that Catholics really can evangelize! I want to persuade other Catholics to get out there and do it—whether on the street or in the regular circumstances of their everyday lives. Jesus Himself has commanded His followers to evangelize (cf. Mt 28:19);

indeed, it is the Church's very mission! Although for some that would be reason enough, I know that many others need extra encouragement and convincing. So, come and see! See what the Holy Spirit is doing on the streets of America, and ask Him what He is calling you to do!

Steve Dawson

Chapter 1

Rescue

Steve Dawson

Detroit, Michigan

I put the car in neutral and slowly pushed it out of the garage into the darkness. It coasted down the driveway and rocked to a stop at the bottom. I took a deep breath, got in, and started the engine, glancing back at the house, expecting to see bedroom lights flick on. Nothing. I gripped the steering wheel and tapped the accelerator. The Thunderbird Super Coupe leapt at my touch, and I managed to persuade my shaking leg to control the gas pedal.

I was thirteen and had never driven before. Some guys at school said they would take their parents' keys and go joyriding at night. This is exactly what I needed, I thought—something different and exciting. I let out a long breath, settled more comfortably in the seat, and flicked on the headlights. This was easy.

After a cruise through our neighborhood, I decided to turn around when I reached our city's main street. Sure, driving was easy, but I had had enough for tonight. I pulled into an empty parking lot, swung a wide U-turn, and was about to reenter the street when I spotted him. My eyes locked with those of the cop in the driveway opposite me. I decided to play it cool and waved him on with my hand. When he waved me on, I snatched the opportunity to get out of there but was careful to maintain the 25 mph speed limit.

He followed me. My heart pounded. Just keep going; he can't stop me if I'm doing nothing wrong. After a few careful turns, I checked my rearview mirror—he was gone. Whew! Flooded with relief and adrenaline, I let the gas have it, and reached 60 mph before managing to screech to a halt at a stop sign. Suddenly my rearview mirror and the entire dash were flashing blue and red.

My only thought: I can't let him catch me! I floored it through the intersection. Before I knew it, the odometer read 120 mph. Suddenly the road began to curve. I knew enough to realize I wouldn't be able to stay on the road at this speed. I stood up on the brake.

The car jerked violently, careened across the road, and slammed into the guardrail. Shoot—he's going to get me now! For several minutes, I tried to restart the car, wondering where the police car was.

Soon it pulled up, no lights, no sirens. The cop got out and approached my car with a flashlight. I rolled down the window, looked him in the eye, and said, "What seems to be the trouble, officer?"

He yanked my little punk self from the car, handcuffed me, and let me have it: "What the hell are you doing? You can kill someone driving like that!"

It was then that I saw my dad's car—nearly cut in half, the backseat fully exposed, gasoline pooling underneath.

My parents met us at the police station at 3 A.M. They were livid. The officer explained what happened, noting that he had cut off pursuit because the chase had gotten too dangerous, and when he saw the car, he expected me to be dead. When my parents asked if they could take me home, the officer said, "No, I think he would be safer spending the night in juvenile detention."

OUT OF CONTROL

I grew up in Bloomfield Hills, an upper-class suburb of Detroit, Michigan. I was the oldest of three children of an unbaptized father and a nominally Catholic mother. My dad was a successful lawyer who worked long hours. Although I received the early sacraments of the Catholic Church, my family's Mass attendance during my childhood was spotty, and I had very little formation in the faith.

When I was ten or eleven, my mom began "searching", and she would drag my sister and me to a different Protestant denomination's worship service each Sunday. We soon tired of dressing up and sitting through sermons, and one Sunday we protested, "Mom, why do we have to go to that Baptist church? We're *Catholics*!" It's not that we were concerned about preserving our faith; rather, in our minds, being Catholic meant staying home on Sunday mornings.

I was something of a "wild child" and grew less and less satisfied with healthy modes of entertainment. At twelve, my friends and I would soak tennis balls in gasoline, light them on fire, then roll them down the grassy hill next to the railroad tracks. In middle school I stole hood ornaments from cars for the thrill of it and was promptly expelled from the only Catholic school I had ever attended. I was a student there for less than a year.

My run-in with the police the night I totaled my dad's car did shake me up a little, but not enough to keep my feet on the straight and narrow. I craved excitement, and as it turned out, bad things tended to feel more exciting than good ones.

In high school, I probably spent more time in the principal's office, in the parking lot breaking into cars, or at the local Pizza Hut than in class.

Once, I excused myself from class to use the bathroom. I took a cherry bomb and set it at the base of a toilet, having attached the unlit end of a burning cigarette to the fuse. My plan for a time-delayed explosion worked perfectly. I was sitting "innocently" in class five minutes later when—BOOM! The fire alarms went off, and everyone evacuated the building. By the end of the day, I was called down to the principal's office.

"Look, Stephen, we know it was you. If you admit right now to having blown up the toilet, you will be suspended. If you deny it, you will be expelled. The choice is yours."

I was really ticked off. He didn't have any evidence! No one saw me, and I didn't tell anyone I had done it, but nevertheless I was indicted by my reputation. It was one of out of nearly a dozen times that I was suspended.

In high school I was enthralled with the party crowd and became heavily involved in alcohol, marijuana, and other recreational drugs. I was officially expelled senior year but received special permission to attend evening adult-education classes in order to get my diploma. This suited me fine since I could sleep in and was able to smoke unhindered during breaks from class.

Growing up, I really never gave God a thought. My behavior and lifestyle were not a matter of rejecting my faith outright; religion simply was not on my radar. What did interest me was the next high, the next thrill, the next girl. I was not violent or aggressive, just generally oblivious about or indifferent to how my actions impacted others.

When I was in high school, my mother's religious search bore fruit, and she had a reversion to the Catholic faith, largely due to the influence of Servant of God Rev. John Hardon, S.J., with whom she had developed a close friendship. As could be expected of a mother who had a son like me, she prayed daily for my conversion and urged me to live a godly life. She had Masses said for me and asked many of her friends, including Father Hardon, to pray for me also. I was not at all interested in her Catholicism stuff, and I rejected the idea that religion could be of any relevance, especially if it meant giving up a "good time".

Fed up with my uncontrollable behavior, my parents threw me out of the house when I was seventeen. I moved in with a friend whose mother was rarely home. After finishing high school, I bounced around from job to job—everything from pizza delivery to construction.

In my early twenties, I actually began to consider my future, but in secular terms only. I might want to get a decent job one day so I could make some money; college might be a good idea. I took classes at Oakland University in Rochester, Michigan, and began to apply myself, yet still maintained my party lifestyle.

At twenty-three, I met Kelly. We hit it off, and I agreed to move with her across the country to Portland, Oregon, where she had been accepted to law school. I was also attracted by the West Coast's party scene, which I had heard beat Detroit's, hands down. I decided to enroll at Portland State University as a business student. After several months, my relationship with Kelly soured, but we put up with each other, since we were both over two thousand miles from home. After about a year, my partying increased to the point that I stopped attending class. Kelly kicked me out of our apartment, and after a month of homelessness, I was arrested for not returning the rental car I had been living in. After a week in jail, the charges were dropped, and I returned to Detroit and moved back in with my parents.

It took me a few months to recover from the detrimental lifestyle I had assumed in Portland, but once I was on my feet again, I jumped right back into the ways of the world. I moved to downtown Detroit where I lived in a loft right next door to a casino and worked as a computer repairman in a pawn shop.

One weekend, my buddies and I took a road trip to Cedar Point Amusement Park in Ohio. On the way home, we were drinking and soon got pulled over. I was the driver, and as the police officer arrested me, he said, "You need to get Jesus in your life." Ha! He sounded like my mom! Why would anyone talk to a complete stranger about *Jesus*? I vowed to report the cop for talking about religion while on duty. My driver's license was suspended, and I found myself living with my parents once again.

A SHOT IN THE DARK

I continued to drink and party, but grew less and less satisfied with my life. Here I was almost thirty, with no real job, a deteriorating body from years of substance abuse, and an empty, gnawing unhappiness. For most of my life, I had done basically whatever I wanted to do. I had catered to the desires of my body for pleasure, and of my mind for highs and thrills. I had been arrested a dozen times for various incidents, mostly involving reckless behavior. I had stolen from my parents, broken into cars, and shoplifted. I had lived for myself, looked out for Number One, taken full advantage of the pleasures this world flaunted. Yet, I was miserable.

Restless, afflicted, and nearing desperation, I found myself open to things I had previously written off. My mother, who had never stopped praying for me, continued to encourage me to turn to God. Figuring I had nothing more to lose, I began to research different world religions, although I pointedly steered clear of the Catholicism my mother professed. My father had recently been catechized and baptized by Father Hardon, and I did not want anyone to come after me next.

It was in the midst of this search that I hit rock bottom. I was sick of my empty life. Suicide flickered across my consciousness as a viable option. I couldn't go on living like this. It was then that I made a challenge to an unknown God, the last-ditch effort of a man whose self-styled life was not working.

I remember kneeling in my parents' backyard, letting the wetness of the grass seep through my jeans. I set down my bottle of Jack Daniels, looked up at the sky, and prayed the first real prayer I had ever prayed: *God, if You're real, You'll have to show me.*

As always, God was faithful. He answered my prayer in two ways. First, He gave me an incredible thirst for the truth and the drive to find it. With this grace, I continued my world religions research with renewed vigor. I scoured the Web, examining Islam, Buddhism, Hinduism, Christianity, like so many clear stones, holding each up to the light, trying to pick out the real diamond from among the counterfeits. I inevitably gravitated toward the religion professing a God of three co-equal Persons, One of Whom took on human flesh and was slaughtered by those He came to save. The undeniable historicity of the Gospels and the logic that Jesus was Lord—as opposed to a liar, lunatic, or simply a wise teacher—won out. Once I accepted the truth of Christianity, God's grace together with honest historical research quickly led me to turn away from the thousands of Protestant denominations and to focus on Catholicism, the religion truly founded by Jesus Christ. Only Catholicism was present during *all* of the Church's two-thousand-year history. Much to my chagrin, the religion I *didn't* want to be true, the one my mom always seemed to be pushing on me, turned out to be the goal of my intellectual search.

An intellectual conversion to Catholicism is not synonymous with a moral conversion to Catholicism. Consider Saint Augustine, who submitted intellectually to the truth of Catholicism, yet prayed, "Lord, make me chaste, but not yet." Similarly, I was getting drunk while watching EWTN. At some point soon, I needed to make a decision. It was very clear to me that accepting Catholicism was an all-or-nothing proposition. Was I willing to give up the life of total self-indulgence that I had lived for nearly three decades? Was I *able* to give it up?

This is where God's second answer to my prayer came in. Once I made a decision to embrace Catholicism intellectually *and* in my moral life, God took over.

Since the age of reason, I had chosen myself over others and God. I had been steeped in habitual mortal sin for years. Now, suddenly, I had the desire *and I was able* to detach myself from these deeply ingrained patterns of sin. BAM! God shattered the chains of my bondage.

I was given a superabundant amount of grace to "reject Satan and all his pomps and works". God enabled me to see sin as the filthy, odious cancer that it is. There is no other explanation for the ease with which I abandoned drinking, drugs, and my overall hedonistic lifestyle. God's deluge of grace blasted away my desire for these things. I can only look back in awe and gratitude at that blessed, graced time in my life.

NEW DIRECTION

A month after my prayer challenge to God, I went to confession for the first time since second grade. My confession took an hour and a half, and the priest gave me the penance of praying thirty Rosaries.

As you can imagine, my mom was ecstatic. This little Saint Monica and her circle of prayer supporters had paved the way for my own feeble prayer to reach heaven and shake down the graces necessary for my conversion.

I got a job working in construction for my uncle. My driver's license still suspended, I rode my bike to 6:10 A.M. Mass before work each day. I paid a coworker to pick me up in the morning and gave him additional money to listen to Catholic radio instead of hard rock on the way to the construction site.

Now that I knew Catholicism was "it", my thirst for the truth grew, and I delved into Scripture and books on theology and apologetics. I devoured works by Frank Sheed, Scott Hahn, Karl Keating, and Patrick Madrid. I read the *Catechism of the Catholic Church* and the three volumes of *Faith of the Early Fathers* by William A. Jurgens and even started to plow through Saint Thomas' *Summa*. I downloaded hundreds of hours of podcasts from the EWTN archives.

The more I learned about the Church, the more captivated I became. I hungered for all things Catholic. I started attending Bible studies at my mom's church, Saint Hugo. Soon after, I asked the associate pastor there, Father Charles Fox, to be my spiritual director. Father Charlie had taught several of the Bible studies I attended, and I was impressed by his spiritual insight.

For about a year after my conversion, I would remember mortal sins that I had forgotten to confess at my "big confession". Whenever this happened, I would simply mention these sins the next time I went to confession. Once, when I confessed a few of these forgotten mortal sins to a priest I didn't know, his reaction startled me. He groaned and lamented, clearly agitated, repeating several times, "That is terrible!" I thank God that this severe reaction did not turn me off to everything he had to say, because the priest gave me some very wise instruction. "You must do penance! And I don't mean just three Hail Marys. You must make reparation! You must fast!"

God's grace allowed me to see the wisdom and fitness of the priest's counsel. Indeed, I had severely offended God, and although the thirty-Rosary penance of my big confession was not easy, it was pretty trivial compared to my offenses against God. So I began to do penance. For over a year, I consumed only liquids on three days a week. With the approval of Father Charlie and my medical doctor, the next Lent I did a complete bread-and-water fast. For months, I slept on the hardwood floor with a shoe box as a pillow. I placed a pebble in my shoe to be a continual source of irritation.

I am not trying to brag by relating these harsh penances, but simply to highlight the unmistakable action of God's grace during this time in my life. I did not find these penances difficult. God gave me a keen awareness of the hideousness of sin and powered my ability to make reparation for my past wicked life. Today, I would find it nearly impossible to sleep on a hardwood floor; I would even complain about being in a regular bed and having one pillow instead of two. But in the year or so after my conversion, that superabundant grace fueled and supplied all my efforts to reject sin, grow in holiness, and make reparation for the evil I had done.

During one of my spiritual-direction sessions in Father Charlie's office, I told him, "You know, Father, since my conversion, I have virtually no temptation to sin in the ways that I used to. I'm not saying I'm perfect or anything—I still have to fight against selfishness and try hard to be charitable, and I know I fail—but the sins I used to be into all the time, I'm just not drawn to them anymore. For example, I have no temptation to lust at all."

Father Charlie raised his eyebrows. "Well, that certainly is not the experience of most people. It seems that God is working in your life in a very powerful way, preserving you from the pitfalls of your past life."

At some point, however, I felt God begin to retract that particular grace that preserved me from the temptations of my past. Over time, my clear sense of sin waned, and God allowed me to experience those temptations again. I started to have to work harder to avoid sin. At first, I was worried that I was doing something wrong or that God was not pleased with me. However, a priest friend told me that God permits temptations because He wants to give us the opportunity to do something for Him—in a sense, to prove our fidelity. If God is doing everything, and we are doing nothing, then we are not fully able to show our love for God, and there's no merit to our good actions.

I compare my situation during that time to a person recovering from a long, serious illness. At first, he must depend on others to do everything for him—push him in a wheelchair, prepare his meals, feed him, bathe him, dress him, and so forth. If he is truly to get better, however, he must begin to do things for himself. He needs to practice walking to strengthen his legs and undergo physical and occupational therapy to relearn to do the activities he could not do during his sickness. In my recovery from a long, serious, spiritual illness, the Divine Physician at first held my hand almost tangibly and made life very easy for me. However, on the timetable He determined to be best, He took away my wheelchair and allowed me to get stronger by more fully experiencing the reality that is part of every sincere Catholic Christian life: the struggle against sin.

I am utterly grateful for God's custom-designed attention to me! And, of course, for His never leaving my side. He is there in the midst of temptations, even if I don't always sense His presence.

As is often the case when one has a major conversion, I had to leave most of my friends behind. I now craved community—authentic, Christ-centered community. Where could I find this? What were good, faithful Catholics involved in? I was eager not only to make friends, but also to do Catholic things, make my whole lifestyle Catholic.

One evening, I attended a Holy Hour of Eucharistic Adoration, and afterward, a woman approached me and made me an invitation that changed my life.

"A group of us plan to meet outside of the abortion clinic on Southfield Road to pray for an end to abortion. We will be there for one hour every day for forty days. Would you like to join us?"

This was the beginning of my work in the pro-life movement. I dove in headfirst. Here was evil, raw and festering. Men and women were duped into having a "medical procedure" to have their baby killed. Grandparents were paying money for the slaughter of their grandchildren. My heightened sense of sin bristled and recoiled at this sheer wickedness, and I was determined to do what I could to snuff it out.

Ten of us prayed outside the abortion clinic every day for forty days. The next spring we organized an official 40 Days for Life campaign, in which people signed up to pray at the abortion clinic in shifts for twenty-four hours a day for forty straight days. That campaign was exhausting! We tried to advertise at parishes near the abortion clinic, but it was often difficult to get pastors on board with the idea. Many hours in the middle of the night were left unclaimed, so my friend Mike Stack and I volunteered to take them.

On Saturdays, I also started to sidewalk counsel women who were making their way from their cars to the building of the abortion clinic. This was draining, intense, and emotionally charged work. Women sobbed and yelled. Boyfriends threatened. I persisted, utterly convicted that I must try to stop the monstrous atrocities being committed in that building.

It was so clear to me that our culture was dying. Not only were babies being killed, but so were the souls of women and men. And I knew it wasn't just abortion that marked our culture's demise, but a whole cesspool of immoral filth. By God's undeserved grace, I had been pulled from this mire, and I knew it was my duty to try to rescue others, too.

OUR LADY'S "SILVER BULLET"

As a newly revived, on-fire Catholic, I was ready and willing to heed the Savior's mandate: "Go therefore and make disciples of all nations" (Mt 28:19). I started with my family and coworkers. This was not the easiest territory. First, it was awkward, but I was willing to put up with that. Second, it didn't seem to bear much fruit. I got the feeling that people thought that I, the great and holy Steve, was looking down on them. Third, I only had so many family members and coworkers.

I began to look for other ideas. I remembered hearing about Saint Maximilian Kolbe, who used to evangelize strangers by offering them a blessed Miraculous Medal. He felt that, as a sacramental, the medal was a channel of grace, our Lady's "Silver Bullet", and God could use it to bring about conversion in a person's life. Saint Maximilian's use of the Miraculous Medal as an evangelizing tool was inspired by the story of Alphonse Ratisbonne.

Alphonse Ratisbonne was a nineteenth-century, anti-Catholic agnostic who was challenged by a friend to wear a Miraculous Medal and to recite daily the Memorare, a prayer to the Blessed Mother. Ratisbonne agreed to the challenge figuring that there could be no harm in patronizing a silly Catholic "good luck charm". Ratisbonne's friend quickly asked some fellow Catholics to pray that God would work powerfully in Ratisbonne's life. The very next day, the Blessed Virgin Mary appeared to Ratisbonne, who readily converted to Catholicism. Within two weeks, he was baptized, and later he became a priest.

I was sold! I decided to try Saint Maximilian's method. I ordered a bulk package of one thousand Miraculous Medals, asked a priest to bless them, and kept a handful in a small pouch in my pocket.

The method I employed was simple. When I was at the grocery store, a gas station, or any public place, I would pick a stranger and casually ask if he would like a free Miraculous Medal. Most of the time, the answer was no, and I would answer, "Okay, no problem, God bless you", and walk away. Sometimes, however, someone would become curious and accept. As I gave the person the medal, I would say, "Here you go. The Blessed Virgin Mary appeared to Saint Catherine in 1830 and promised that whoever wore this medal would receive great graces from God. So many miracles occurred because of it that it became commonly known as the Miraculous Medal."

Typically, the responses to my spiel were positive and short: a smile, a "thank you", or maybe a hearty "Great! I'll take any miracles I can get!" Occasionally, people would tell me something they were struggling with and ask for prayers. Once in a while, someone would decline the medal after hearing what it was, but usually people were pretty receptive. Once, in the check-out line at a plant nursery, I asked the cashier if he would like a Miraculous Medal. To my surprise, he nonchalantly stuck his hand down the collar of his shirt and said, "I just wanted to check if I already had one on here." He held out his scapular.

Most of the time, I never saw the people who received my medals again and never knew if they wore the medal, chucked it in the back seat of their car, or promptly threw it in the nearest garbage can as soon as I had turned my back. I did know, however, that my offering of the medal was a way to open up the conversation to what really mattered in life: the spiritual realm. And, of course, the medal was a blessed sacramental. In God's design, in His Catholic Church, material things play an important role in sanctification and worship: bread and wine, holy water, incense, sacred chrism, the laying on of hands, to name a few.

After all, the second Person of the Blessed Trinity took on *flesh*. I had no doubt that in God's economy a blessed Miraculous Medal could serve as a conduit of grace in a person who had an ounce of openness or desire. Just as Saint Maximilian said.

My most significant encounter involving the Miraculous Medal happened one evening when some friends and I attended a sidewalk-counseling training session. After the meeting, we went to a nearby diner to socialize and discuss what we had learned. I decided to give our chatty, young waitress a Miraculous Medal.

"I have a present for you," I said. Being a good sport, she held out her hand, and I dropped in a Miraculous Medal. I told her the story behind it and asked, "Are you a Christian?"

"Yes, I go to Trinity Baptist Church two miles up the road."

"That's great! Have you ever thought about becoming Catholic?"

The waitress hesitated. "Yes, my boyfriend's Catholic, but I'm not sure I agree with everything Catholics believe."

I inquired further, and she cited a few areas of contention with the Catholic Church, including the Church's teaching on abortion. Naturally, everyone at the table had something to say in response, and, to her credit, our friendly, open-hearted waitress engaged us in dialogue.

Then she left to tend to other customers. At the end of our meal, I felt compelled to give her a model of a baby at ten weeks gestation, a pro-life pamphlet, and a Rosary, all of which one friend had in her car. The waitress accepted them willingly, and on our way out, we all promised to pray for her.

Three months later, my friends and I attended a second session of sidewalk-counseling training. I suggested we go back to the same diner and visit "our favorite waitress". When we arrived and it turned out that she was working that night, we requested her section, and she immediately recognized us. After we were seated, she handed us menus and told us that she had some news. A few minutes later, she sat down right next to me in the booth.

"When you guys came in a few months ago, I had just found out I was pregnant. I was going to have an abortion, but after talking to you that night, I knew that God sent you as a sign for me to keep my baby. God gave me the courage to tell my boyfriend and my mom about my pregnancy. I am now six months along, and they are so supportive of me keeping the baby!"

We cheered and congratulated her. I couldn't resist, "You're going to get that baby baptized, right?"

I JUST MET A GIRL NAMED MARIA

As I continued to use the Miraculous Medal as an evangelization tool to try to bring others to God, God continued to work in my own life. I felt Him nudging me to do something even more drastic, to give even more of myself to Him. I began to discern a call to the priesthood and religious life. After much prayer, spiritual direction, reading, research, and a "Discernment Weekend", I decided to enter the Franciscans of the Immaculate in Bloomington, Indiana. I was slated to enter the community in August 2009. Then I met Maria.

She had been organizing a pro-life campaign at our parish, and I had volunteered to help. We soon found ourselves working on the same pro-life projects, and within a couple of months, we acknowledged that we were starting to have feelings for one another. However, Maria was also discerning a call to the religious life and was to enter a community of sisters in September. Several months before her entrance date, Father Charlie advised that we cut ties. It was very hard, but we knew it was the right thing to do.

After fourteen months of life with the Franciscans, I discerned, with the help of my superiors, that God was not calling me to a religious vocation but rather to life in the world. I left the friary in May 2011. Around the same time, I discovered that Maria had come to a similar conclusion about her own vocation and was back at home!

Maria and I dated all that summer, and one evening in late September I proposed. I had had lunch with her father just that day and asked for her hand. I did not want to waste any time, but I didn't yet have a ring. We were kneeling in front of the tabernacle, when I turned from our Lord to Maria, asked her to be my wife, and in lieu of an engagement ring, I gave her—you guessed it—a Miraculous Medal. (Don't worry—she got her diamond the next week.)

Chapter 2

Birth of a Movement

Steve Dawson

Portland, Oregon

The day after our wedding on March 24, 2012, Maria and I started the five-day, 2400-mile trek from Bloomfield Hills, Michigan, to Portland, Oregon, in a Ford F150 pick-up pulling a U-Haul trailer. On a Friday afternoon, we arrived at the one-bedroom apartment I had picked out online. The following Monday I started class as a senior finance student at Portland State University, where I hadn't set foot since I was a doped-up son of this world over ten years before.

On the day I asked for Maria's hand, her dad asked me a question. "So, Steve, are you planning to finish college?" I assured him that if it was God's will, I certainly would, and when a small business I was running for my uncle folded a few months later, I decided it was now or never.

Although Michigan has a fine array of universities, I figured it made the most sense to return to Portland to finish school. Portland State University held three years of my college credits, and although moving across the country is no picnic, I would face losing a year of credits if I were to transfer to a new school. Maria and I planned to spend a year in Portland while I finished my degree, and then return to Michigan where both our families lived.

So here I was, a newlywed and thirty-six-year-old college senior living three time zones from home. The past year of my life had been a whirlwind. Within a mere year's time, I had left religious life, moved from the Franciscan friary in New York to Michigan, dated Maria, run a small business, gotten married, moved from Michigan to Oregon, and gone back to college. It's no surprise that I was preoccupied and slightly stressed, and my evangelization efforts ended up on the back burner.

"PREACH THE GOSPEL ALWAYS"

Maria and I sought Catholic fellowship in our new city, and so one Friday night about a month after we had arrived in Portland, we attended a showing of an episode of Father Robert Barron's *Catholicism* series at the Newman Center at Portland State University. After viewing the DVD, the participants divided into small groups for a structured discussion.

The third or fourth question the small-group leader put to us was, "How do you evangelize?" I felt a twinge of guilt, considering that I hadn't given anyone a Miraculous Medal in the past month. The person sitting across from me answered readily, "Like Saint Francis—'Preach the gospel always, and only use words when necessary.'"

Others at the table nodded in agreement, and one woman said, "Yeah, if you go to Mass and are kind to people—just being a good Catholic, basically—you shouldn't have to say anything. You'll be witnessing to others just by the way you live."

I inwardly cringed, and as the discussion continued around the table in a similar vein, I questioned whether I should say anything. When it was my turn, I scraped together all the charity I could muster.

"Well, actually, did you know that Saint Francis never said, 'Preach the gospel always, and use words when necessary'? I learned this when I spent over a year discerning a religious vocation with the Franciscans. It always bothered us when people would attribute that quotation to Saint Francis because if you look at his life, you see that he was constantly preaching the gospel *with words*. It was his holiness of life that gave power to his words. While the saying may have some truth, we have to be careful not to use it as a cop-out and think that we're evangelizing just by being good people."

To his credit, the guy who said the alleged Saint Francis quotation took my counter amiably in stride. The discussion soon ended, and Maria and I said our good-byes, but that brief conversation on evangelization stayed with me.

I kept thinking that we as Catholics have the fullness of the truth, yet we are so hesitant to share it with others. We have real good news, the best news anyone could give—how to save your soul and gain eternal blessedness—yet we keep it to ourselves. Further, Jesus *told* us to share that good news—"make disciples of all nations" (Mt 28:19)—and we don't! We have a mandate from God, and we are too scared, lazy, lukewarm, unbelieving, ignorant, busy, fill-in-the-blank to obey Him. As far as I could tell, Protestants and even *non-Christians* such as Jehovah's Witnesses and Mormons do much more active evangelization than Catholics do, and they don't even have the convincing power of the fullness of the truth to stand on. What's the problem with us Catholics?

Later in the week, I shared some of my thoughts with Maria at dinner.

"When was the last time you were out somewhere, in a public place, and a stranger tried to talk to you about the Catholic Church, tried to evangelize you?" I asked her.

"Well, never, I guess."

"Right. It's never happened to me either, because Catholics aren't doing it. But why not? I mean, Jesus told us to preach the gospel to all nations. It's not an option; that's what we as Catholics are *supposed* to be doing. Evangelization is part of being Catholic."

"What about you and your Miraculous Medals?" Maria said. "That's Catholic evangelization."

"Yes, and I need to be doing that more. I've totally slacked off. Giving out Miraculous Medals is great, but sometimes I'm just not motivated. I know I should force myself to give them out, but sometimes I still don't. I need to be doing something more consistent. We should be going out in public, at the Saturday Market for instance, and just talking to people about the Catholic Church."

Maria looked at me. "Yeah, we could evangelize at the Saturday Market," she said slowly. "But I would be terrified."

The Saturday Market is a large art fair that takes place every Saturday and Sunday, April through December, in a park in downtown Portland on the banks of the Willamette River. The area has lots of foot traffic, as well as street performers and food vendors. Many people come for the fair itself, and others are out jogging, dog walking, or biking on the paved path along the river. Kids gather to play in a fountain springing directly from the pavement. The atmosphere is busy but relaxed. No one is rushing off to work, and folks seem content to while away an afternoon, sipping bubble tea and browsing through pottery and silk-screened T-shirts. Would they also be willing to undertake a more serious "browse" through their own spiritual inventory by engaging in a conversation about religion?

For the next week, I continued to ask my friends the question I had posed to Maria: "Have you ever been in a public place and seen Catholics evangelizing?" Their answers were universally no. They had seen Bible-waving Protestants, bicycling Mormons, and smartly dressed Jehovah's Witnesses, but no Catholics. The more I considered this, the more determined I became to do something about it. The prospect of doing Catholic evangelization at the Saturday Market intrigued and excited me. More than this, I felt called by the Holy Spirit to try it.

It was in a conversation with a friend named Nick that my idea began to move forward. Maria and I had met Nick at a gathering for young adults at Holy Rosary Church where we started attending Sunday Mass. I knew Nick was serious about his faith and was very interested in apologetics. When I asked him if he had ever seen Catholics publicly evangelizing and he gave the expected negative response, I followed up with, "Why don't we go do it?"

"Awesome! Where?"

"Why don't you come over for dinner next week and we'll discuss it?"

AN IDEA TAKES FLIGHT

The following week, Nick brought his friend Katelynn to our apartment for dinner and an evangelization meeting. After meatloaf and asparagus, I laid out my idea: we would go to the Saturday Market; set up a table with Catholic pamphlets, Rosaries, and Miraculous Medals; and talk to people about the Catholic Church. The four of us became animated as we brainstormed the nuts and bolts of how it would work. How would we attract people to us? A megaphone? No, too impersonal and in-your-face. A sign? Great—what should it say? We threw around ideas about the wording for the sign and finally settled on the following:

Catholic Truth

Got questions?
Free literature
Need prayer?
Find true joy!

We chose images of the Sacred Heart of Jesus and the Immaculate Heart of Mary to accompany the text.

We could get pamphlets from the backs of Catholic churches and the Newman Center. I would ask a 40 Days for Life friend from Detroit for some Rosaries. I still had a small stash of Miraculous Medals, and I would order more. Katelynn knew of a sign shop owned by Catholics, and Nick volunteered to pay for our sign. Each finalized detail stoked our excitement, and we agreed to go to the Saturday Market the first Saturday after the sign was ready.

In the meantime, I called the city to find out what kind of activity was allowed in public parks. I knew I had free speech, but there might be some simple regulations that it would behoove us to respect. I learned that we could not sell anything without a permit, we could not erect a structure, and we could not impede the flow of foot traffic. The limits were no big deal; our free speech remained unhampered.

On a Saturday late in May 2012, not even two months after we had moved to Portland, Maria, Nick, Katelynn, and I set up shop as the first would-be St. Paul Street Evangelization team. Just outside the Saturday Market, we spread out a picnic blanket on the concrete, erected the "Catholic Truth" sandwich board sign, and set out Rosaries, pamphlets, prayer cards, and Miraculous Medals. Then we sat down, prayed a Rosary, and waited for people to approach—and for the Holy Spirit to do His work.

Many people passed by, some ignored us, some read the sign then quickly looked away. Others stopped and simply wanted a prayer card or a Rosary. One of us, usually Nick or I, would engage the person in conversation and try to find out if he were Catholic. Most of the conversations were short, positive, and sincere, and they enlivened me. I packed up that day with the joy that comes from sharing Christ, a keen sense that this is what I was supposed to be doing, and the confidence that, yes, we could actually do this!

I was hooked. Maria and I went out every Saturday, and usually Nick and Katelynn joined us. Our day would start with 9:00 A.M. Mass at Calaroga Terrace Senior Living Apartments (the latest Mass we could find on a Saturday morning), then we would pack up our materials and head to the Market, where we would often evangelize for as many as five hours. Sometimes other members of our Catholic young adults group would join us.

Over the weeks, we slightly modified our approach. Instead of just waiting for people to walk up to us, we began to offer free Rosaries to passersby. This technique was helpful in that it drew attention without being too obtrusive. If someone declined or ignored us, we did not push the matter. This approach also broke the ice for those who were interested but hesitant to talk to us. And, of course, many people are attracted to anything that's free, especially kids who would pull their parents toward the strings of colorful beads.

I was amazed at how receptive and open many people were to talking about religion—especially Catholic Christianity.

Portland, Oregon has a reputation for being artsy, tree-hugging, dog-loving, and politically and socially liberal. The city's unofficial motto, proudly plastered on many car bumpers, is "Keep Portland Weird", and I'm convinced a considerable part of its population is striving to do just that. Some of the weirdness is healthy uniqueness. Eight architectural masterpieces span the Willamette River, connecting the city's east and west sides. Portland has an abundance of thriving small businesses, including the most microbreweries of any U.S. city. It has the highest percentage of bicycle commuters of any major American city. And some of the weirdness is just plain quirkiness. Native Portlanders don't bat an eye at the man wearing a kilt and Darth Vader mask, riding a unicycle through the park while playing the Star Wars theme song on flame-throwing bagpipes. Some of its weirdness, however, is downright unsavory. Portland has the most strip clubs per capita and is host to one of the largest World Naked Bike Rides every year. It is home to Voodoo Donuts and the 24-Hour Church of Elvis. It's been said Portland is one of the nation's least churched cities.

For this reason, I expected a lot of hostility and snotty remarks. Sure, there was the man who muttered, "Catholic Truth—that's an oxymoron", as he passed our set-up. There was the lady from Eastern Europe who yelled at us because she blamed the problem of the world's poverty on supposed overpopulation caused by the Church's stance against contraception and abortion. Another time, a woman who had published a book with a blasphemous title about how the Catholic Church scarred her, and in which she sought to offer healing to other "afflicted" Catholics, set out boxes of her books, free for the taking, just several yards from our "Catholic Truth" sign.

But, really, these types of responses were few and far between. The majority of our encounters at the Saturday Market were with people who were polite and interested. About half the people we talked with were lapsed Catholics. We always encouraged them to return to regular Mass attendance—but to confession first, of course. Many showed some sign that they were inspired to return to the sacraments and walked away with a "How to Make a Good Confession" pamphlet. Non-Catholics of all stripes also stopped by our set-up. Nick once had a discussion about Christ's institution of the papacy with a pair of young Mormons who were themselves out evangelizing. Before they left, they accepted a CD of a talk by Peter Kreeft called "Seven Reasons to Become Catholic".

On another occasion, a Protestant couple admitted to me that they had been confused by all the contradictory doctrines taught at the various churches they had attended. I agreed that this was a huge problem, held up my Bible, and asked, "But we know what the pillar and bulwark of truth is, right?"

"Absolutely. Of course, it's the Bible."

I smiled and said, "That's the most common answer, but that's not what the Bible itself says. Let's look at 1 Timothy 3:15." I flipped open my Bible. "This verse calls the *Church* 'the pillar and bulwark of the truth.'" The couple was intrigued, and as I explained to them that Christ founded not a Bible but a Church which is visible and authoritative, I could see that their wheels were turning. I gave examples of how the Fathers at the early Church councils looked to Scripture *and tradition* to settle doctrinal debates and stamp out heresy. After half an hour of discussion mostly focused on the founding and authority of the Church, the couple departed with pamphlets on twenty different Catholic topics. As they walked away, I praised God for their openness and prayed that it would continue when they sat down to read our literature.

Although we did engage in our fair share of apologetics while out at the Saturday Market, we also encountered many people who needed something else. Once Nick and I spoke with a man who had recently lost his job and felt that he had hit bottom. After talking with us for a few minutes, he commented, "I think God meant for me to find you guys today." We explained to him that God had a plan for his life, and it included a relationship with Jesus Christ and His Church. We gave him a copy of the short book *Made for More* by Curtis Martin and my contact information, encouraging him to call me for further discussion. Sincerely thankful, he promised to read it.

SPROUTING SEEDS

We knew that, for the most part, we were planting seeds. We did not expect to see many—or any—on-the-spot conversions. Spurred on by the rhetorical questions of Romans 10:14, "And how are they to believe in him of whom they have never heard? And how are they to hear without a preacher?" we were putting the Word out there, allowing It to be heard. We were planting seeds and trusting that God would see to the rest.

But sometimes we were blessed to witness the germination of a seed and even see a tiny shoot push its way through the soil.

One Saturday in late September, a planted seed took root before our eyes. From our usual set-up just outside the Saturday Market, I could see a man watching us from a distance. He was about my age, mid-thirties, lanky, wiry, his black tank top allowing full view of his heavily tattooed neck and arms. As he approached, I noticed piercings in his nose and eyebrow. He stopped in front of our picnic blanket.

"Would you like a free Rosary?" I asked from where I knelt on the blanket, Rosaries and pamphlets arrayed before me.

"Yes, I really would." His reply was earnest and slightly sad.

As I extracted one Rosary from a pile of others, I asked the usual follow-up question put to any Rosary-taker. "Did you know that the Rosary is a prayer?" He nodded.

"Are you Catholic?"

The man dropped to a squat to be at eye level with me. "I know I was baptized a Catholic and made my First Communion, but I'm not sure if I can be considered a Catholic anymore."

"Do you go to Mass?"

"I did a little as a kid, but my parents really weren't into it. They stopped going early on. Actually, my dad was in prison, and my mom was pretty much out of the picture."

I could tell he wanted to talk, so I asked the big question. "So, now that you're an adult, why don't you go to Mass on your own?"

He laughed softly and shook his head in incredulity at the suggestion. "I don't think I could—or should. I mean, it wouldn't be right for me to." Then he told me his story. It was tragic, but one that I knew was not unusual. He had been raised with little parental guidance and no other role models. At an early age, he experimented with drugs and sexual activity. The experimentation developed into habit, and now he found himself in a lifestyle that no kid ever aspires to. What was different about this man, however, was that he seemed to feel some sense of the tragedy of an ill-spent life.

I decided to pull out a second big question. "If you were to die today, where do you think you would end up?"

He gazed at the river behind me and said slowly, "I know I would go to hell."

"But you don't have to!" I said, impressed by his honesty. "God is merciful. He loves you. He wants you to be with Him forever. He wants you to come back to Him." Then I told the man my story—my sinful life, my cry out to God, His superabundant mercy and grace, the new joy-filled life I now have as a Catholic Christian living my faith. I shared with the man, whose name I learned was Joey, the basic gospel message, the good news of salvation. God created us to be in relationship with Him, but we have ruptured that relationship through sin. Jesus, God's Son, repaired our broken relationship by dying for our sins and rising from the dead. We have access to this restored relationship by having faith, repenting of our sins, being baptized, and committing ourselves to live fully for God in His Church.

"And, Joey," I said, "do you want to hear even more good news? You already have the 'baptized' part down. Your next step now is to repent of your sins and confess them to a priest." Big question number 3. "Would you like to get right with God and go to confession and Mass with me? You won't regret it."

"Yes," he said simply, "I'd like that." Joey and I exchanged contact information, and then he left. As I packed up our materials, I praised God for the action of the Holy Spirit working in our conversation.

Later that evening, I called Joey to give him the details about Mass the following morning. He answered on the second ring and took down the time and place.

"I live quite a distance from there, and I'll have to take the bus," he said.

"No problem," I said, "but try not to be late. After Mass, we can ask Father John to hear your confession."

Actually, I had my doubts about whether Joey would show up the next day. I had gotten this far with other people I had talked to at the Saturday Market, and they ended up being no-shows. And I know how hard going to confession after thirty years can be, not to mention facing the reality that an essential part of the sacrament is the resolve to amend your life.

But when Maria and I pulled into the church parking lot the next morning, there was Joey, sitting on the front steps.

The Mass was long, nearly an hour and a half. I kept worrying that it would be too much for Joey, but my sidelong glances told me that, if he wasn't actually praying, he at least seemed attentive.

It was the practice of Father John to meet with people privately in the sacristy after this last Mass of the day, people who sought his counsel or wanted confession. No appointments were necessary; people simply waited in a room adjacent to the sacristy. Maria and I had met with Father John before and knew that the wait could be as long as an hour. Again I was worried about Joey's tolerance, but he did not seem fazed by the extra time. Finally it was our turn, and Joey and I entered the sacristy.

"Hi, Father," I said. "This is my new friend, Joey."

"Joey, welcome! What brings you in today?"

I told Father John how we had met and allowed Joey to unload his story. It was clear that Joey was disgusted and unhappy with his life, but he was also wrestling with attachment to sin. He listed several behaviors and asked Father John if he would have to give each one up.

"And what about a little marijuana, Father? Like just on the weekends?"

"No, Joey, you don't need that stuff anymore."

Joey finished his questions and became quiet, taking it all in, all that this new life would entail.

"Father, Joey would like confession," I said.

"Joey, is this true?" Father John asked.

Joey nodded, and I took my cue to leave. Half an hour later, the sacristy door opened, and Father John waved me in. Joey stood up, radiating a peaceful smile, and thanked Father John. We were about to leave the sacristy when Father John called out, "Good-bye, Giuseppe."

Joey turned and said, "Hey, how did you know that I was baptized with the name Giuseppe?"

Father John shrugged. "I just knew." Then he smiled thoughtfully and said, "A new name for a new beginning?"

Joey looked at the priest and nodded. "Yes, I am now Giuseppe."

Giuseppe and I left the church, two men with lightened, renewed hearts, awed by the movements of the Holy Spirit and the mercy of the Father. As Giuseppe headed to the bus stop, he turned and called out to me, "I'll see you next week."

We did see Giuseppe at Mass the next week and then again at First Friday devotions. Since then, we have lost touch with him, but we know he is in our Lady's hands. Praise God for running to meet all the prodigal sons of this world!

SPREADING THE GOSPEL ... SPREADS

Our encounter with Giuseppe happened on the tails of a summer that had seen street evangelization take off as no one expected.

From the very beginning of our presence at the Saturday Market, I knew this work was something I wanted to share with others. I do not mean to say that from the beginning I envisioned an official nonprofit organization with employees and a country-wide membership. Rather, I was simply convinced that the Holy Spirit was working through us as we evangelized, and we were doing in a concrete, literal way what the gospel demands of Catholic Christians—to preach the gospel to the whole creation (cf. Mk 16:15). I wanted other Catholics to embrace this gospel expectation as well, and I was eager to share with them a way I knew was effective.

I did a couple of things to help spread the word about what we were doing. First, I called some Catholic friends back in Detroit. Simple as that. They loved the idea, and although it took a little time for them to get organized, they became the second evangelization team.

The second thing I did was to post captioned photos of our Saturday Market evangelization on Facebook. I had not been a big Facebook user up to this point, but I knew the potential audience extent, ease, and popularity of using Facebook, so I made sure to post pictures every weekend. I even established a Facebook page just for Catholic

Street Evangelization, and the day we got one hundred followers, we were ecstatic.

Facebook did what it does best—connect people (and take up a lot of my time!). People and their friends and *their* friends responded to our photos and captions with delight, affirmation, and praise to God. Although I appreciated their encouragement, my hope was that the pictures and stories would spur them to action of their own. Despite this hope, however, I was surprised when people began contacting me and asking, "How do we do what you're doing?"

To me, it seemed simple enough. Find some like-minded Catholics and a public place, take a few sacramentals, and go to it. Did they really need me to take them through it step-by-step? Of course I was happy to do it, but as more people got in touch with me with the same request, I began to realize that the process of beginning street evangelization really may not be as clear-cut as I thought.

So I directed inquirers to the websites where I ordered my pamphlets, Miraculous Medals, and the custom-made "Catholic Truth" sign. I agreed to ship some of them Rosaries, since I was still getting a steady supply from my Rosary-making contact in Detroit. And, of course, I answered questions, questions, and more questions. No, you don't need to ask anyone's permission to evangelize, but just check your local ordinances about what you can set up in a public park. Yes, it's a great idea to pray with someone, but just be sure to ask him before you start. No, we never use a megaphone, because we want to be nonconfrontational and allow people to choose to listen to us.

It soon became clear that we needed to raise some money if we were to continue street evangelizing like this. For the first few months of our life in Portland, Maria and I lived off our wedding gifts and our savings while we settled in and Maria looked for employment. Then in mid-June, Maria found a decent office job, and I was able to work part-time doing maintenance at our apartment complex. Still, I was a student, and we didn't have a lot of money to throw around.

Giving away hundreds of Rosaries, pamphlets, and Miraculous Medals every weekend became expensive. We had started to order pamphlets from various Catholic publishers, since you can conscionably take only so many free pamphlets from the backs of churches. We requested reimbursement for shipping costs from the new teams to whom we sent Rosaries, but I would not refuse anyone who didn't have the funds.

One evening, Nick, Katelynn, Maria, and I met with the Director of Evangelization for the Archdiocese of Portland. He was excited about what we were doing and very encouraging, but that was all he could give us from an archdiocese that had just emerged from bankruptcy. We were on our own.

Our first boost came when friends from church, Dirk and Allison, gave us one thousand dollars. With this generous donation we were able to purchase enough materials for two evangelization stations, including a healthy supply of pamphlets, and still have some buffer money left over.

Throughout the summer, we continued to evangelize every weekend, each day unique, never uneventful. A couple of times, habited Dominican brothers and priests joined us, and Father Francis even heard confessions right there on the waterfront. Nick and I made friends and had lengthy conversations with a man who was at the Market almost as much as we were. He wore a large sign that read, "The end is coming. Are U Saved?" On the Fourth of July at the Blues Festival, Maria took a break from evangelizing to telephone our families in Detroit to announce that she was pregnant.

We weathered the Gay Pride Festival, occurring on the same stretch of river as the Saturday Market, which was also the same day as the World Naked Bike Ride. (Good ol' Portland.) That afternoon two rainbow-decked women approached our picnic blanket.

"We're lesbians. Are you guys here because we're here?" one of them asked, waving her hand in the direction of the Gay Pride Festival.

"No, we actually had no idea the festival was going on. We're here every Saturday," Maria answered. "You're welcome to some literature or a medal. Everything here is free."

The woman gave the blanket a cursory glance. "Does the Catholic Church hate gays?" she challenged.

"No, not at all," Maria shook her head vigorously. "The Catholic Church loves everyone and teaches that every person is to be treated with respect and dignity."

"Okay, then, so what does the Catholic Church think about homosexuality?" the woman asked.

"Well, the Church teaches that same-sex attractions are not wrong in themselves. It's the homosexual acts that are sinful. But, again, the Church teaches that people with same-sex attractions—like all people—are to be treated with love," Maria said.

The two women actually seemed genuinely interested in what the Church had to say, but also gave us reasons why they considered their lifestyle to be right and normal. The exchange was friendly, but it was cut short when the women left to watch the Naked Bike Ride that had just started. We tried to do what Maria just said: love these misguided children of God with the heart of Christ. We hoped we had planted a seed by "speaking the truth in love" (Eph 4:15).

ST. PAUL STREET EVANGELIZATION

In August, we named our blossoming apostolate "St. Paul Street Evangelization" after the great Apostle to the Gentiles and consecrated it to Our Lady of Guadalupe, Patroness of the Americas and Star of the New Evangelization. That same month news of what we were doing seeped beyond Facebook into other regions of the virtual world. A Catholic convert from atheism, Leah Libresco, interviewed me for an entry about St. Paul Street Evangelization on her blog on *Patheos*. A few days later, in an online article for *First Things*, Elizabeth Scalia quoted from the Libresco blog post, describing our nonconfrontational approach to evangelization. After the description, Scalia commented, "I think of Jesus sitting by a well, or a healing pool, and striking up conversations with the people who crossed his path. It's a street evangelization I can get behind."[1] Yikes! She just compared us to Jesus. Those are big shoes to try to fill.

By the end of the summer, St. Paul Street Evangelization had ten teams of evangelists in ten different U.S. cities. I continued to field calls and e-mails from interested Catholics, walking them through the basics of setting up their own chapters. By Christmas 2012, we had twenty-five teams.

I just kept putting one foot in front of the other, and it was as though the organization grew itself. A need arose, and we responded to it. For example, in trying to outfit itself, a new team faced going to five different websites to order materials—too laborious and expensive. To streamline this process, SPSE purchased all the supplies more cheaply in bulk, and then sold the items from one website. I was even able to buy sign faces

[1] Elizabeth Scalia, "Evangelization Is Meant to Persuade Not Provoke", *First Things* "Web Exclusives", August 21, 2012, http://www.firstthings.com/web-exclusives/2012/08/evangelization-is-meant-to-persuade-not-provoke.

a hundred at a time, purchase wood and hardware separately, and build the signs myself for much less than the cost of complete, premade signs.

Also, in response to countless requests for evangelization training, we published a series of pages on our website, describing our non-confrontational approach and outlining some basic practical guidelines to evangelization, such as how to find common ground and be a respectful listener. Later we would develop a complete online Basic Evangelization Training course.

Another need was for inexpensive pamphlets pertinent to our work of street evangelization. The pamphlets we had been giving out on the street were designed for Catholics to take from the backs of churches or for teaching apologetics to Catholics, not for street evangelization, and, to purchase these, a team would have to buy a minimum of fifty pamphlets per topic. If they wanted pamphlets on twenty-five different topics, for example, a team could face spending hundreds of dollars. So we launched a pamphlet project, involving many theologians and apologists who wrote and edited tracts on thirty different topics, with the express intent for them to be a resource for the street evangelist. We made these available to download digitally so that teams could print the materials they wanted for free.

We managed to reduce the start-up cost for a team from over five hundred dollars to less than two hundred. Of course, no team was under any obligation to buy anything from us, but if they chose to, they would be getting their materials as cheaply as possible.

You could say that the organization grew organically; as we perceived a need and tried to meet it, SPSE developed accordingly. Or, more accurately, you could say the Holy Spirit was behind the whole endeavor, directing our movements and decisions, giving shape and purpose to our work.

The Holy Spirit was working on my own heart and mind as well. As I continued to evangelize people on the street and to guide other Catholics in doing the same, I became more interested in what the Church herself teaches about evangelization. When I read Pope Paul VI's remarkable Apostolic Exhortation *Evangelii nuntiandi*, it resonated within me. In it, the Pope writes, "Evangelizing is in fact the grace and vocation proper to the Church, her deepest identity. She exists in order to evangelize."[2]

[2] Paul VI, *Evangelii nuntiandi*, On Evangelization in the Modern World, December 8, 1975 (Washington, D.C.: United States Catholic Conference), no. 14.

Yes! Evangelization is the Church's deepest identity! It is the *reason* Jesus instituted the Church! He wants *all people* to have access to those life-saving sacramental graces that, in God's plan, are bestowed through the Church. He desires to save all people—so He instituted the Church. That is her mission, that is why she exists—to bring everyone into her fold, offering each one salvation. As part of the Church, as members of Christ's Body, we are bound to embrace that mission. We are bound to evangelize.

And the need to evangelize has become urgent. In *Redemptoris missio*, Pope Saint John Paul II writes, "God is opening before the Church the horizons of a humanity more fully prepared for the sowing of the Gospel. I sense that *the moment has come to commit all of the Church's energies to a new evangelization*.... No believer in Christ, no institution of the Church can avoid this supreme duty: to proclaim Christ to all peoples."[3]

I first felt this urgency when after my conversion I started to undertake our Lord's work.

My pro-life work several years prior had brought me face-to-face with an evil that was destroying babies, women, men, families, and souls. I had been fighting it on the front lines—the sidewalk before the entrance to the clinic of death. But why were women even showing up here in the first place? What was it that caused them to make an appointment to kill their babies? How could we prevent *that*?

Now I saw much more clearly that abortion, monstrous as it is, is just a symptom. It is a symptom of the disease of Godlessness. All the evils of our society—abortion, pornography, divorce, promotion of the homosexual lifestyle, unbridled permissiveness in the name of "tolerance", contraception, fornication, the list goes on—are manifestations of a culture having turned its back on God. Our culture is sick, even dying, because its Source of health and life has been abandoned. You could fight any one of these evils directly, but it would be like trimming the leaves off a weed, or even taking a lawnmower to it, but not yanking it out, root and all. I saw that the solution to the evil of abortion—or any of these evils—is simply to destroy the root. Bring God back.

These evils are like the moles in the old arcade game, Whack-a-Mole. A mole head pops up in one corner of the game board, and as soon as you

[3]John Paul II, *Redemptoris missio*, On the Permanent Validity of the Church's Missionary Mandate, December 7, 1990 (Washington, D.C.: United States Catholic Conference), no. 3 (emphasis added).

whack it down, another pops up somewhere else. You keep whacking at the moles, and new ones keep popping up. *Whack, pop! Whack, pop! Whack*—while you're fighting gay so-called marriage, *pop!*—legislation mandating the teaching of homosexuality to kindergarteners appears. What we really need to do is unplug the machine. Bring God back.

Of course, God has always known that society's moral evils are a symptom of His absence in men's hearts, and from eternity He has planned a solution: His Church. Evangelize. Bring God back.

And here was Pope Saint John Paul II calling for *all of the Church's energies* to be devoted to evangelization. I was on board! I wanted St. Paul Street Evangelization to serve the Church's core mission, full force!

Please understand that, although I was certain that destroying the root of the disease was the best way to cure the body, I realized that the symptoms needed to be addressed, too. I had every respect for people who prayed outside abortion clinics, sidewalk counseled women, wrote their legislators about moral issues, promoted Natural Family Planning, and did every other proactive, positive measure to fight the symptoms afflicting our culture. They were containing the evils, helping to prevent their spread, helping to prevent sin. But what I was feeling called to do was to target the root of our cultural disease; I wanted to bring God back.

WHAT DO YOU WANT OF US, LORD?

At the beginning of 2013, I came to a crossroads. I was due to graduate in March, just a couple of months away. The expectation, of course, was that I would seek a job in my field like every other college graduate on the planet. Yet, here I was already working thirty-five to forty hours a week pro bono for the nonprofit organization that the Lord had used me to found in spite of myself. I couldn't imagine working full-time at a regular job *and* managing SPSE on the side, *and* being a husband and a father to the little one due at the end of the month. I had to make a decision.

I felt strongly that St. Paul Street Evangelization was where God was calling me. It seemed that His hand was guiding us the whole way. I didn't move to Portland to start an evangelization organization; I came to finish school. I didn't plan for my evangelizing efforts at the Saturday Market to be the start of a nationwide movement; I was just trying to take my gospel call seriously. By God's design and providence, SPSE was born. Could He want it simply to fizzle out, as would probably happen if I moved on to a job in finance and no longer had the time to counsel new team leaders, ship resources all over the country, promote the apostolate, maintain our social-media activities, manage the volunteers who wrote pamphlets, and continue to street evangelize as well?

If God had taken us this far, I had faith that if it was His will that SPSE continue, then He would provide a way. Maria and I prayed about the situation, and I spoke with my spiritual director. After several serious discussions, Maria and I agreed on a plan: after graduation, we would move back to Michigan and live with my parents (who had offered many times to house us). We would give it six months. We trusted that in that amount of time God would make His will clear. If not, then we would pack it up and say, "Well, I guess that's not what God was calling us to do", and continue our own evangelization efforts on a small scale.

In April, Maria and I moved back to Detroit with our two-month-old son, Maximilian. Although my parents kicked me out at seventeen, they have graciously taken me back in many times, and this time with my little family.

Through God's grace and guidance, SPSE continued to grow. More and more people responded to the Holy Spirit's prompting to live their baptismal call to preach the gospel to the whole creation by way of street evangelization. SPSE teams continued to sprout all over the country and even beyond, and, as an organization, we were blessed to reach several key benchmarks, including the IRS's tax-exempt 501(c)(3) status. By the six-month mark, Maria, my spiritual director, and I concurred that it indeed appeared that St. Paul Street Evangelization remained in God's plan for us.

God had used my "Portland Disaster" of years ago as a launch pad for the take-off of a movement that would allow us and our fellow evangelists to glorify Him. I was humbled to be a part of it and prayed that I did not get in the way. I was continually blown away by the zeal of faithful Catholics, fueling the organization's growth, and I struggled to keep up. As I put in more and more hours to run St. Paul Street Evangelization, one thing became clear: I needed help.

Chapter 3

Prodding Each Other Toward Heaven

Adam Janke

Lansing, Michigan

I stretched my arms into the air in the swivel chair where I sat in my office at Saint Mary parish in Williamston, Michigan. Whew! Today—like all days at my job as the Director of Religious Education—I had work up to my ears.

I would jokingly tell others that, as the DRE, I was the "Director of Religious Everything". I was in charge of or assisted with elementary, junior high, and high school faith formation, youth group, adult faith formation, sacramental formation, Rite of Christian Initiation of Adults and Children, baptismal preparation classes, catechist recruitment and formation, and I was the point man for the Protecting God's Children program. I served on our evangelization, education, finance, and worship commissions, served on our pastoral council, helped our school with faith formation, helped pave the way for a functional Catechesis of the Good Shepherd Program that is now a model for other parishes, ran the Vacation Bible School, organized Festival of Praise nights and trips to Steubenville Youth Conferences, assisted on our diocesan youth-ministry committee, and managed our diocesan trip to the National March for Life. I built and maintained our parish website and e-mail system and helped with a lot of the tech needs around the parish. Occasionally, I would also put together events such as *Laus Deo*, a summer program with youth concerts and speakers.

Yes, I was busy, but I loved my job and was overjoyed and honored to be serving the Church.

At that moment, however, the old brain needed a rest, and I clicked open my standby for two-minute office breaks, Facebook.

Scrolling through vacation photos of my friends' kids, I did a double-take at one posting. I couldn't believe it—Catholic street evangelists? I clicked on the link and brought up the Facebook page for "St. Paul Street Evangelization". I began to read what this group out in Portland, Oregon, was doing to evangelize people on the street, bringing people to *Catholicism*. Unbelievable! It was a "light bulb" moment. Of course! Why weren't we doing this as Catholic parishes? So many "welcoming" and "evangelization" committees in Catholic parishes stop at the parish door. I felt that we were severely falling short by not going out and sharing the gospel with our neighbors and community. That had always frustrated me, but here was a chance to be really involved in direct evangelization. I read further and was thrilled that this was something anyone could do. I could invite my parishioners to participate, even without extensive training.

I did not need another activity on my plate, but this street evangelization was something I could not pass up.

I had been involved in Church work for six years as a DRE and youth minister and felt as if so many of our Catholic parishes were stagnant. In my experience, certain Catholic Church employees and priests seemed to be living out their vocations and work as a business instead of as a ministry. It was as if they had forgotten the great promises of the New Testament and were living for committee reports, parish statistics, and financial data instead of devoting their lives to the gospel. I must admit that once in a while I would catch myself falling prey to this mentality, too. I knew that our very identity as a Church is to evangelize, but instead of focusing on spreading the gospel, it seemed we were too often caught up in the details of parish business life. So I was ready—yearning—to bring the living gospel to living people, directly, not through any committee or program. And here was a way, so basic, so obvious, so personal.

I immediately sent an e-mail to Steve Dawson, the guy who started St. Paul Street Evangelization. Within a day, we talked on the phone, and I was on my way to starting an SPSE team for Lansing, Michigan. That was in August 2012, and in September a small group of parishioners and I began to "preach the gospel to the whole creation" (Mk 16:15) right out on the streets of our town. We evangelized in downtown

Williamston and then at Michigan State University. My experience was like that of so many others—what I thought street evangelization would be and what it actually ended up being were two different things.

I thought it would be a lot of doctrinal debate. I thought most of the people we met would yell at us since the media gives such a poor account of the Catholic faith. Instead I found that most of the people we talk to are just like us—friendly, good people. But they are broken and need Christ. Many were receptive to our message and offers of free Rosaries and pamphlets. Once, I was even thanked by a Protestant evangelist for doing street evangelization as a Catholic.

I love the opportunity that street evangelization provides to have a personal encounter with these people—to tell them the God who created them out of love has an awesome plan for their lives, and that that plan hinges on Jesus Christ.

By God's design, we humans need and rely on each other. We are instrumental in one another's lives. In Romans 10:17, Saint Paul says, "So faith comes from what is heard, and what is heard comes by the preaching of Christ." This means that someone has to be doing the preaching! One person has to be sharing the gospel in order for another person to hear it and embrace it. And, of course, all this occurs within the mysterious matrix of the workings of divine grace.

I have seen this work itself out in my own life. I was not always Catholic, but God put people in my life to "preach" to me and lead me to Him and His Church.

FROM CATHOLIC TO LUTHERAN TO BAPTIST

I was born and baptized into the Roman Catholic Church. Like many young Catholic public-school children, I attended CCD classes. All I remember about Mass at this time is that I would sit behind another kid from the neighborhood, and he would turn around and talk to me—well, at least until we both got in trouble. I was not the most reverent six-year-old at Saint Alphonsus Catholic Church.

Around this time, my mom, who was single, met my soon-to-be dad, and when they got married I was taken out of the Catholic Church, and we became Lutheran. My mom told me that she was very angry with the Catholic Church for something bad that had happened and was more than happy to become Lutheran because it was close enough. At my age I followed my mom where she went. It seemed to me that the Lutheran Church wasn't all that much different than the Catholic Church. Everything about it was still boring to an eight-year-old who did not understand what was going on. As far as I was concerned I was missing Sunday morning cartoons. Mighty Mouse was waiting at home, and I was stuck on an uncomfortable pew only half interested in what was going on so I could know how much longer before the whole ruckus would be over.

By the time I was in high school, I had warmed up to religion a little and became increasingly interested in the Scriptures. I wanted to reread some of the Bible stories I remembered from my childhood—Noah and the Ark, Daniel and the Lions' Den, and Moses and the Ten Commandments, to name a few. I decided to dig a little deeper and figure out what was between the stories I knew so well. I even brought my Bible to math class as a help in warding off boredom.

As I grew more interested in the Scriptures, I was also more attracted to going to church, and I began to get involved. I became an acolyte in our Lutheran church (one of those kids who lights and extinguishes the candles at the beginning and end of the service) and a lector, and then volunteered as the liturgical assistant, who played a major part in Sunday worship. I signed up every chance I could get, sometimes twice a month, at times leaving little room for others. The older folks in the church didn't seem to mind one bit, seeing someone so young so excited about helping in the worship service.

One day a student who sat next to me in class noticed my Bible. Eric asked me if I would be interested in attending a Bible study held once a week at the school and said he would be happy to introduce me to everyone. Oh, and there would also be refreshments. Now food was one thing that I couldn't refuse.

This Bible study and visits to a Baptist church were the beginning of my split with the liturgy of our Lutheran church. The Baptist church focused more on biblical interpretation during the service, and that is what I was into. I also loved the praise and worship. These elements were attractive enough that I wanted to visit more Baptist churches to see if they were similar. I was on a church quest. I ended up visiting several Baptist, Methodist, and Christian Reformed churches, and even threw in a visit to a Catholic church for the sake of fairness. I finally settled at North Park Baptist, making the decision to become Baptist formally and to be rebaptized.

A particular event helped solidify my decision to become a Baptist. Eric from math class had invited me to go on a mission trip to Dayton, Ohio, where we were to help a local pastor evangelize at his newly planted mission church. We stayed at the church that night, and the next day as we were on our way to lunch, Pastor Mann suddenly stopped the parking-lot attendant and asked him if he knew he was going to go to heaven if he died right then. As I recall, the poor man looked terrified, as if someone were about to mug him. The pastor led the man through the "Roman's road to salvation", a series of verses from the book of Romans that Protestants use to explain the gospel message. Then Pastor Mann asked me to pray the "sinner's prayer" with him. I wasn't even a Baptist yet, but I stumbled my way through it. That confrontational experience of street evangelization was something I definitely tried to avoid in the future. Still, the overall experience of the mission weekend was positive, and I grew in friendship with the others on the trip. I felt that I could be vulnerable with them about my own questions and feelings about the Bible and faith. It was in the context of these relationships, marked by a commonly held set of doctrines that I began to embrace as my own, that I decided to give my life to Jesus Christ in a deeper way and made the decision to become Baptist.

After a few years I married my high school sweetheart, Teresa, and became a full-time employee in the nationwide distribution center of Family Christian Stores. I was content to be a Baptist till the day I died.

TAKING ON THE CATHOLICS

I spent a majority of my free time reading and contributing to an online Baptist message board. My favorite forum on the board was the "Other Denominations/Religions" area. And my favorite pastime was debate. A large variety of people visited this area of the message board—from those who practiced Wicca to people who were quite close to the Baptist faith. And we had a couple of Catholics.

The Catholics particularly interested me. I had come from a Lutheran background and now understood what was wrong with that faith, so it seemed it would be easy to bring these Catholics, whose faith I assumed was so close to Lutheranism, to an understanding of what the Bible said, and convert them.

The Catholics that came to our Baptist board were brave souls, something I have always given them credit for. They were by far outnumbered and were up against some highly intelligent Protestant scholars, some of whom seemed to specialize in anti-Catholicism. I myself tried to take the approach with these Catholics that I was there to listen to them and their stories, to show friendship, and to try my best to teach what was written in God's Word.

As I began to challenge the Catholics who came to the forum, and they responded with an astute understanding of the Holy Scriptures, I, like so many others before me, quickly discovered that the stereotypes I had been taught about Catholics were simply not true. I realized that Catholics do not worship statues or Mary as I had once thought they did. They do not believe that the Rosary is a magical charm, or that the scapular will automatically save them from hell, or that the pope is sinless.

As my false ideas about Catholicism began to dissolve, I knew I had to find out—just what is it that Catholics actually believe? In God's providence, I had at my fingertips some of the most intelligent, faithful lay Catholics in the country. This included one young man named Carson Weber, who was studying at the Franciscan University of Steubenville for his master's degree and was an assistant to one of the most popular Bible teachers and theologians in the country, Dr. Scott Hahn. At the time I didn't know just how intelligent these young Catholic men and women were, but I would quickly learn.

Carson and some other Catholics from the forum did me an incredible service—in the form of a challenge. I had told them that I wanted to go to seminary to become a pastor, and they challenged me to be intellectually honest in my views and teaching about the Catholic Church. In other words, it would be acceptable for me to disagree with Catholic doctrines as long as I knew the truth of what I was disagreeing about and was upfront in my explanations of it.

Carson and his friends put their money where their mouth is. One day I discovered on my porch a sizable package that had been sent to me by these Catholics. It contained a plethora of books—many by Scott Hahn, a *Catechism of the Catholic Church*, some works by Pope Saint John Paul II, and others. These resources greatly aided my quest for intellectual honesty, and after tearing through them, I started scouring the used-book shelves at Barnes & Noble, hunting for the well-known spine of Ignatius Press volumes and Catholic authors I was interested in.

TIPTOE IN THE TIBER

This is, perhaps, how a turning toward the Catholic Church happens for many people. They find out that some of what they thought about the Catholic Church is not true, and in a call to intellectual honesty will attempt to correct others who assert the false views. They find themselves actually defending the Church when they are yet apart from the Church and disagree with many of her doctrines. This is exactly what I found myself doing.

A Catholic whom I met on the Baptist forum, Dustin Sieber, invited me to his online Catholic forum to continue my education. He openly warned me, however, that those who frequented this website tended to end up converting to the Catholic faith. I laughed and said, "Uh-huh, sure", and visited the website, Phatmass.com, anyway.

In addition to improving my doctrinal understanding of the Catholic faith, Phatmass gave me a cultural education. I met many wonderful, humble Catholics who showed a solid level of commitment to and faith in Jesus Christ. Some of these had relationships with Christ deeper than I had ever seen before in any church. It was truly humbling to my own soul. They had something I desired strongly—a depth and unity to the Christian faith I had never experienced before in any sacramental or reformed church. Part of me felt that perhaps this just might be the answer to the discontent with the denomination-jumping I had thus far lived with.

After a while I was banned from the Baptist message board for teaching in defense of Catholicism even though I was still opposed to the idea of any Protestant becoming Catholic.

AN EXPERIENCE OF MASS PROPORTIONS

One Saturday, I showed up for an evening Mass, not really sure what I was doing there, but hoping that maybe if I sat through a Mass again, some answers would click into focus. I chose a pew in the back of the church, and Bible gripped to my chest, I watched everyone file in slowly. As they entered their pews, people knelt and made the Sign of the Cross. There was very little talking before the service started. How odd. Even when I was a Lutheran I remembered that everyone fellowshipped before the liturgical services. In this case, however, all eyes were on the front of the church—toward the cross.

Suddenly music started, and the priest walked to the front of the church with the lector and two altar boys. He made the Sign of the Cross announcing, "In the name of the Father and of the Son and of the Holy Spirit", and greeted the congregation. Nothing really seemed amiss so far. As a Baptist I believed in the Trinity. If Catholics chose to identify themselves in God's name, that seemed all right.

Then the priest led the people in a time of confession. I expected the priest to say, "I forgive your sins", but he surprised me by saying, "May almighty God have mercy on us, forgive us our sins, and bring us to everlasting life." Wait a minute! Not only was this completely biblical (cf. 1 Jn 1:9), but it made perfect sense for a time of confession to be found in the context of worship. Also, the priest didn't declare it his power to forgive sins as God, but instead pronounced the words of forgiveness in place of Christ who is now seated at the right hand of the Father. Jesus wasn't there to say, "I forgive your sins", so the priest was telling the people exactly what Jesus was doing when they repented and confessed. It was as if the priest were acting in the place of Jesus, mediating His presence. Why didn't Baptists take time in their worship to ask for the forgiveness of sins? That only happened if someone was going up to be saved.

As I looked around during the Eucharistic Prayers, I noted that these Catholics seemed intent on what they were doing—worshipping God. The focus seemed to be on the cross, and then, heads bowed, on the priest and the altar, then back to the cross. After the priest welcomed the congregation forward to receive Communion, they returned to their pews and knelt again in worship. I could not read their hearts, but it sure seemed that they truly believed Jesus was with them and present in the meal they had just partaken. Some cried, some knelt or sat silently, some glowed with soft smiles. As for myself? My heart melted. Even in the suffering of my denominational indecision, there was joy.

I prayed, "God, if this is true, if what is happening here today is the same thing that happened two thousand years ago in the upper room, then I want to be part of it. Give me the wisdom and knowledge to come home. But if this isn't what You desire, if what is taking place here is wrong, all the quicker, by any means necessary, call out to me, bring me out." I have known joy in my Baptist church. There was a great deal of fun and fellowship, there was faith in Christ, and there was an emphasis on the Bible. But there still seemed to be things missing, such as a certain reverence for God and a liturgy that took its meaning and structure right from sacred Scripture.

Going to Mass didn't really solve my dilemma. In fact, it seemed in a way to make it worse. My problem would have been solved if I had seen blatant paganism or idol worship. Instead, I saw people worshipping only God, giving praise to Jesus Christ for what He had done for us, and all in a service saturated in Scripture.

SUDDENLY, ANGELS

From that time on I started attending Mass every Sunday. It was, after all, more biblical than a Baptist service. I found myself filled after each service. My wife used to tell me, "You always come home from Mass with a smile on your face." One Sunday during Mass I had a thought: if the Catholic Mass is as Baptists and others say it is—the work of Satan—then Satan isn't doing a very good job. We come together every Sunday and fall deeper in love with God, worshipping Him and Him alone. If this is the work of Satan, then he would be doing the very thing Christ told us was impossible: for Satan to cast out Satan.

It also became clear to me that my Baptist church was part of denominationalism. The unity that Christ prayed for in John 17 was missing. The Catholic Church was different, though. In *The Courage to Be Catholic*, George Weigel notes "that the Catholic Church is not a *denomination*—an institution whose form is typically defined by the will of its members—but a *Church*—a community whose basic structure and boundaries are defined, once and for all, by the will of Christ. For the Church is the Body of Christ, and those who are ordained to act *in persona Christi*, 'in the person of Christ,' exercise headship in the Body, the Church."[1] The prospect of finding an answer to the old denomination question was too much to pass up.

[1] George Weigel, *The Courage to Be Catholic: Crisis, Reform, and the Future of the Church* (New York: Basic Books, 2002), p. 26.

I longed to become Catholic, but before making that final decision, I set out to undertake one last round of talking to people, praying, and studying—one last attempt to find something, anything, that might keep me out of the Church. I spent months rereading massive volumes on Catholicism. I reflected on all I had learned on the debate boards, and I prayed a lot. I knew deep down that the Catholic Church was all it claimed to be, but I was just afraid to make the leap. Then, almost completely out of the blue, my lifelong Baptist wife announced to me that she had decided to become Catholic. Say what? I was in complete shock!

As it turned out, while I had spent a great deal of time studying, Teresa had spent a great deal of time listening and learning on her own as well, at first on how to drag her husband out of his heresy. Like me, however, she learned that she could not be completely fulfilled and truly united to the Body of Christ outside the Catholic Church. She, too, had decided to sit through a Mass, intending to poke holes in it, but when the priest elevated the Eucharist, she just saw Jesus calling her home.

That was enough for me. I was ready to come home, too, and I was ready to announce it. So I shared with the world that I would become Catholic.

THE MOMENT OF TRUTH

Teresa and I attended RCIA classes together. Several months after we began, a great weight crippled my soul. I knew all about mortal sin and realized that a sin I had recently committed fit into that category in every way. I went to the pastor of the church, Father Don Lomasiewicz, a wonderful Polish priest, and explained to him my situation and that I desired the sacrament of penance. It must have seemed quite odd to him to have someone so young who was still in RCIA in his office asking for the sacrament. He understood my plight, however, and had me right then and there make an act of faith first, to reconcile me to the Church, and then he helped me through my confession. There I confessed to the Lord all that I had done that was displeasing to Him, and listened as Father Don offered the words of absolution.

It was a powerful moment. It was sacramental. God made a promise. He told us to confess to one another. He gave the power to bind and loose to the apostles. And now, here, in this pastor's office, I had heard it all aloud. The confessional is a place of healing. It's the doctor's office of the soul. The first few times I went to confession I completely broke down into tears, barely making it through the Act of Contrition. And indeed it was very healing. Never before had I been so sorry for my sins, because I had displeased God who had done so much for me, and never before did I feel so free from those sins, so healed, so deep in my relationship with the Lord as I did at those times. I believe if all Catholics truly understood what took place in the confessional, most churches would require a confessional to be open almost perpetually.

Teresa and I made our First Communion together a little while later. That Sunday, the priest announced to the congregation that it was our First Communion, and we went up first and received Christ, the Bread of Life. That was in 2005, and today we remain happily Catholic with a growing family. We know we are at home now, and the nagging feeling that there is something "more" in worship is gone.

As I look back on all the people who assisted me on my journey home to Catholicism—Eric from high school (albeit unwittingly), Carson Weber from Steubenville, Dustin Sieber from Phatmass, my wife Teresa, Father Don, and so many others—I see even more clearly that, by God's design, we are communal persons who are meant to help each other. And the biggest help you can give is to prod another person toward heaven. Jesus has told us to preach the gospel to the whole creation because no one can find the good news of salvation inside himself. We need to hear it from others, then take it into ourselves, always relying most on that indispensable ingredient, grace. The gospel is meant to be shared—that's why Christ instituted the Church. Community support is essential to who we are as humans; evangelization is essential to who we are as Catholic Christians.

My relationship with Jesus Christ and His Church is the most important thing in my life. Even after becoming Catholic, I continued to study the faith, always yearning to dig deeper and expand my understanding of the Church's rich truths. I attended Franciscan University of Steubenville and earned bachelor's degrees in Catechetics and Theology and a master's degree in Theology and Christian Ministry. I knew I wanted to work for the Catholic Church to give my full support to this beautiful institution founded by Christ and to lead others to love Christ and the Church as I do.

FROM SAINT MARY TO ST. PAUL

So here I was as the busy-beyond-belief DRE at Saint Mary with this St. Paul Street Evangelization phenomenon taking a larger and larger role in my life. And I welcomed it.

The month after my first experience doing Catholic street evangelization, I found myself involved in SPSE in a way I had not anticipated. Steve had posted on Facebook that SPSE was to have its own website by September 30. When that date came and went with no website, I sent Steve an e-mail inquiring about it. He responded that he was frustrated because the company he had hired to build a website had not followed through on its deadline and that getting in touch with them was very difficult.

"I can build one for you," I told him. Since high school, I had dabbled in computer programming and web design as a hobby and had already built a website for my parish. I wasn't a certified professional, but I was sure I could give SPSE what it needed. Steve jumped at my offer, and I managed to take a day off work to get a bulk of the project done.

That was the beginning of my deepening relationship with SPSE. After building the website, I continued to volunteer in other ways. People were asking Steve for some kind of training to help prepare them to evangelize, so I did the research that led to the very first "Basic Evangelization Training". I also volunteered my time to help put that course online with another group of volunteers. Later we put together a second online course, "Catholic Apologetics". Soon after I started this work, Steve asked me to be on the organization's Board of Directors.

In the spring of 2013, Steve began talking about the possibility of having me come on board as an SPSE employee. I thought he was joking at first. It is pretty rare to start a self-sustaining Catholic nonprofit that has more than one full-time employee. SPSE was a baby at the time. I think we were all watching to see what the Holy Spirit wanted for this apostolate.

The timeline for bringing me on board quickly shrank. At first, we talked about two to three years, then two years, then one year, then six months. When I realized that Steve was serious about hiring me and that the proposed start date was quickly moving up, Teresa and I prayed about the decision. We felt that God was telling us that this is what He had been preparing me for in my work at the parish. Even before I discovered SPSE, I had discerned that I was not going to be at Saint Mary for much longer (my plan was to leave by 2016). I had assumed I would get another DRE or diocesan job, but here was the Holy Spirit leading me in a totally fresh direction. I see now that my parish work has proven invaluable because it provides insight into the life of parish ministry and politics, and SPSE is an organization that seeks to build a bridge of trust from the street into the local parish, where Catholics live out their lives from baptism to Funeral Mass. In the late fall of 2013, I became the Vice President and Program Director for SPSE.

BASIC EVANGELIZATION TRAINING

One of my responsibilities is to teach our live Basic Evangelization Training (BET) in dioceses across the country. The day-and-a-half course presents topics such as the New Evangelization, Spiritual Life of the Evangelist, Basic Evangelization Etiquette, Sharing the Story of Salvation, and Practical Apologetics. The course involves prayer, lectures, small-group discussion, and role-playing, and each participant leaves with a BET participant's manual.

The first live Basic Evangelization Training I taught was in my own diocese of Lansing, Michigan. Several weeks after this training, I received permission from the pastor of a nearby parish to try to recruit evangelists from among his parishioners. I had set up a display about St. Paul Street Evangelization in the vestibule of the church and was waiting for Mass to finish. As the closing song began, a few people trickled out, and a man whom I vaguely recognized approached me.

"Hi, Adam," he said. "I'm George Fisher. I attended the evangelization training course you ran a few weeks ago."

"Oh, right. Nice to see you again, George."

"You'll never guess what happened to me," George began. "About a week after I took that course, I was driving on the highway when I saw a car swerve off the road and crash into the guardrail. I stopped to see if I could help and called 911. The guy in the car was pretty shaken up, and I asked if I could pray with him. So we prayed together and even talked about the Church a little bit, and when the ambulance got there I left him my contact info. I know I wouldn't have done all that if I hadn't taken your evangelization class."

"Wow, George, that's great!" I said, genuinely impressed.

"And here's the best part." He paused, and I looked at him expectantly.

"The driver called me the next week," George said. "He told me he used to be Catholic and wants to come back to the Church!"

"That's awesome! You must have been really allowing the Holy Spirit to work through you", I said.

It is a gift from God for me to hear a story like this. It is affirmation that what we are trying to do in the Basic Evangelization Training is bearing fruit in people's lives—in both the evangelized *and the evangelist.* George had certainly taken seriously what he had learned in the class and was courageous enough to apply it. The call to evangelize must have resonated deep within him, as it should for any baptized Catholic who is attuned to the Spirit's movements in his life. I am quite certain that as George continues to look for opportunities to share the gospel with others, he will himself strive to live that gospel message more fully and fall more deeply in love with our Lord and His Church. As he articulates what he believes, he will learn the faith better himself. The more George listens to the Spirit's gentle whisperings, the closer his heart will grow to this Source of all love. In the words of Pope Saint John Paul II, "*Faith is strengthened when it is given to others!*"[2]

Several months after my conversation with George, I led a Basic Evangelization Training in Rochester, New York. At the end of the training, a woman approached me and thanked me profusely for the course. She explained that she was a convert and was lit with fire to share the Catholic faith with others. However, her lived experience in the Catholic Church and especially in her parish did not match the zeal and passion for the faith she had as a convert. She felt disturbed and devastated that most of the Catholics she knew were lax in their faith and saw no reason to evangelize. Having learned at the training that the Church's very mission is evangelization and having witnessed other Catholics take seriously the urgency to share Jesus Christ with others, she now had a new, enlivening sense of hope. She said that it had given her "emotional healing" to take our evangelization training.

The BET is designed with Pope Francis' exhortation in mind: "Every Christian is challenged, here and now, to be actively engaged in evangelization; indeed, anyone who has truly experienced God's saving love

[2]John Paul II, *Redemptoris missio*, On the Permanent Validity of the Church's Missionary Mandate, December 7, 1990 (Washington, D.C.: United States Catholic Conference), no. 2 (emphasis in the original).

does not need much time or lengthy training to go out and proclaim that love. Every Christian is a missionary to the extent that he or she has encountered the love of God in Christ Jesus."[3]

We keep the training short and do not require that our evangelists take it, but we have found that people want training—they ask for it—and that it inspires them to take hold of the graces of their baptism and confirmation and to allow the Holy Spirit to work through them. The training helps give them confidence that evangelization is something they, personally, can actually do. And in the case of the woman in Rochester, it gave her reassurance that evangelization is something she is *supposed* to do.

NOT JUST FOR THE STREET

We purposely don't call the training "Basic *Street* Evangelization Training", because its focus and scope is broader than just evangelizing on the street. The point of the training is to help equip and embolden people to evangelize in all the circumstances of their lives, on the street or not, as George did when he found himself at the scene of a car accident. And we know that an invaluable tool in evangelizing in virtually any situation is the Miraculous Medal.

There's a Subway restaurant that has been a regular stop of mine for years. I know all the employees by name, and they know me. One afternoon as Tanya was preparing my sandwich, she mentioned that she was going to take a month off from work to care for her dad who was dying of pancreatic cancer.

"They're going to try one last treatment," she told me. "It's a surgery called the Whipple procedure. They don't really expect him to make it, but if this surgery works, it'll take him months to recover."

"I'm sorry to hear that, Tanya," I said, as I reached into my pocket. "Hey, I have something for you." I handed her a Miraculous Medal and explained its history and significance.

"Wow! Thanks, Adam!" She hesitated. "Are you sure it's okay that I take this? I mean, you know I'm not Catholic, right?" she asked.

[3] Francis, *Evangelii gaudium*, The Joy of the Gospel, November 24, 2013 (Vatican City: Libreria Editrice Vaticana), no. 120.

"It's totally fine that you have it. Don't worry at all. Give the medal to your dad, and be sure that you pray every day and trust in Jesus to take care of him."

Tanya agreed to pray and thanked me again for the medal. True to her word, she didn't reappear for a month. Then one day, when I walked into Subway, she was standing behind the counter.

"Hey, how's everything? How's your dad?" I asked her when it was my turn in line.

Tanya stopped in the middle of putting on her plastic gloves, looked at me, and smiled. "Adam, the doctors are baffled."

"What do you mean?"

"Well, my dad had the procedure, and he went home after a week," Tanya said. "The hospital called to check on him, and I told them he's doing fine, eating pizza, and drinking a gallon of coffee like he used to. They seemed kind of upset or surprised by that or something. He went in for tests, and the cancer's gone! Yeah, the doctors are baffled. They've never seen such a quick recovery from the Whipple procedure—and with the cancer all gone, too!"

I rejoiced with her and praised God for His goodness and mercy. Is this a bona fide, documentable miracle mediated by a Miraculous Medal? I don't think we'll ever know the answer to that while on earth, but the facts seem pretty convincing. And I can only imagine that the faith of Tanya and her dad have been wonderfully bolstered by what took place, and that is, perhaps, an even greater miracle. Since then, I've encouraged Tanya, who is Christian, to check out the Catholic Church, and I plan to invite her to the "ALPHA for Catholics" program that will be starting at my parish soon. I've joked with Steve that if we just delay the publishing of this book for another six months, we'll be able to report that Tanya is Catholic! I know I'm getting ahead of myself—all in God's time.

Yes, I love to promote the Miraculous Medal. Once, I was invited to give a presentation on evangelization to a small prayer group in another parish in my diocese. Although not a BET, my talk contained the same core message as the formal training. At the end, I gave each participant two Miraculous Medals. I directed my listeners to keep one medal for themselves, and I challenged them to give the other away in an act of evangelization.

A couple of weeks later I received the following e-mail from Christine, a member of the prayer group who heard my presentation:

Hi Adam,

I just wanted to share where the two Miraculous Medals you gave me went. I took one to work with a Rosary I made for a coworker. This woman was baptized Catholic, raised Baptist, and now goes to a Lutheran church. Her fourteen-year-old daughter suffered an assault this summer, so I told the coworker that she may not always be able to be with her daughter, but if she gave her daughter the Miraculous Medal, then she would know that her Heavenly Mother is always with her. I also gave the coworker the Rosary I made and the tracts you gave me, one on how to pray the Rosary and the other on coming back to the Church.

The second medal (the one I was going to keep) I felt the Lord urge me to give to my family doctor today. After my appointment, I gave it to him and told him I felt the Lord wanted him to have it. Well, he started crying and said he's been going through a rough time and the medal came at the perfect time. He kept hugging me and thanking me . . . praise God!!

Christine sent me a second e-mail about a month later:

Here's a follow-up on the Miraculous Medal I gave away. I had another appointment with the doctor I gave the medal to. I was sitting in the waiting room and couldn't believe what I was hearing—Christian radio playing over the speakers! I've been seeing this doctor for more than twenty-five years, and this was definitely a change. When the doctor came in to see me, he was wearing the Miraculous Medal, and he made a point to tell me things were so much better since he received it. Praise Jesus!!

Amen! Christine's e-mail exemplifies an aspect of St. Paul Street Evangelization that brings me much hope: the grassroots nature of this apostolate. It is evident to me from my work in the parish and diocese that ordinary Catholics have a lot of untapped potential in using the gifts God has given them. However, I know the New Evangelization is not so much the work of experts and professionals, but of everyday Catholics responding to God by using the charisms they have been given to advance the cause of Christ. And here is Christine using her gifts of relationship building and sensitivity to the needs of others to bring Christ to people in her daily life. Ordinary Catholics like Christine have made St. Paul Street Evangelization flourish by growing in their faith, opening up to the idea of being pushed outside of their comfort zones, and saying yes to sharing their faith on the street and in the circumstances of their everyday lives.

But it is not just those ordinary Catholics who are at the heart of this apostolate. Pope Francis reminds us that those who take the sometimes uncomfortable and even frightening leap of sharing the gospel do not do so alone: "Though it is true that this mission demands great generosity on our part, it would be wrong to see it as a heroic individual undertaking, for it is first and foremost the Lord's work, surpassing anything which we can see and understand. Jesus is 'the first and greatest evangelizer'. In every activity of evangelization, the primacy always belongs to God, who has called us to cooperate with him and who leads us on by the power of his Spirit."[4]

Let us always rely on Him who sustains our every breath, allays our every fear, and makes marvels out of our lives, "surpassing anything which we can see and understand."

[4]Ibid., no. 12.

Chapter 4

The Valley of the Shadow

Edwin "Uzi" Mendez

Chicago, Illinois

Brooklyn, New York, in the 1970s, where my mother was born and raised, was full of ethnic neighborhoods centered around Catholic parishes. My father was from Puerto Rico by way of Chicago, but moved to New York where he married my mother. I grew up surrounded by the other Puerto Ricans in Brooklyn. Think of the tough kid, hands in pockets, leaning on his back foot with hair slicked down like the gang members in *West Side Story*. My friends called me Uzi, and this is my story.

Even as a child, I could sense my mother's great virtue and faithfulness. My father knew this, too, and he wanted to be the husband she deserved. But as hard as he tried to be a good man for such a good woman, he just couldn't do it. After a while the old restlessness took hold of him, and when I was about a year old, and my baby sister, Grisel, was only a few months old, Dad up and left for Chicago. He went back to his old neighborhood where he already had two young sons by another woman.

Grisel and I were left with a broken-hearted mother who had to work hard to provide for her two babies. For eleven more years my mother tried to make ends meet, despite the crushing struggle and burden of life on her own. Faith, for mom, was a priority and the source of her strength. She took us to Mass, and we received our early sacraments. But the struggle wore her out, and she died when I was only twelve years old. I truly believe she died of a broken heart.

After my mother died, the most important person in my life became Father Rosa, our parish priest. He must have known something of what I was feeling at that time: the heavy sense of responsibility for my sister, my fear, and above all the anger, first at my mother for not being strong enough to hang on, but also at my father. Since I was now old enough to realize fully what Dad had done in leaving us, my heart began to grow hard with the sense of being wronged. My sister and I were fortunate to have an aunt who took us in, but that did not erase the feeling of being abandoned by both parents. It would be a long time before I was able to find the peace I had known with my mother.

Father Rosa was the pastor of Precious Blood parish in Brooklyn. He did everything from calling numbers at the Friday night Bingo to celebrating the liturgy, and he did not tolerate slackers. He also led the youth group, making sure the young men and women knew about the world around them while at the same time preparing them to be strong and faithful Catholics. So when as a teenager I started missing Mass on Sundays, Father Rosa knew it. A good and dedicated priest, Father Rosa went to the families without waiting to be invited. A firm knock on the door could set the heart pumping. Naturally when I heard that knock, I was in no hurry to answer it. I opened the door defiantly, with little attempt at being respectful.

"Uzi, where were you on Sunday? I didn't see you at Mass. You know you need to go to Mass on Sunday!" Father Rosa insisted.

"Well, Father, you know how it is. Things come up," I responded, knowing that such a reply would not go very far. Despite my lack of interest in the faith at that time, Father Rosa still treated me as one of his own. I couldn't help but respect him and depend on him. With his support, the memory of our mother, and sheer grit, Grisel and I made it through those hard times. If it weren't for Father Rosa, I never would have completed my high school requirements. He was the one who kept asking me what I wanted out of life and how I was going to get it. With his help, I was beginning to make something of myself.

As time went on, my sister began to feel the need to reconnect with our father and the little family we had left. So when we were in our early twenties, Grisel decided to move to Chicago, and I followed her, knowing she would have a hard time settling in a new place. Sadly, our relationship with Dad turned out to be like a cold war; we barely tolerated each other.

Louis, however, was a different story. My half-brother and I connected easily, and I quickly came to admire him. What a life he had! His flashy possessions, his fashionable clothes, his wealth and stature were all so attractive, especially after my life of struggle. I soon found out that all his power and fancy things came from being the head of the gang known as the Spanish Cobras. I might have been scared by this, but Louis stayed by my side, introduced me everywhere as his brother, and offered me many luxuries I had never had.

This guy had it all. Besides the material benefits, the gang brought a thrill to my life that I had not experienced before. As the leader's younger brother, I was being groomed to take over one day. At the time I did not think of the consequences of being a gang leader because my brother was not old, and we both assumed that he would be around for a long time. I just coasted along and didn't pay much attention to the harsher realities of gang life.

Imagine my shock and fear when Louis was diagnosed with terminal cancer. It was fear for my brother, but also for myself, and the life I would have as the Cobras' leader. Slowly I was beginning to see through the glamour to the violence and despair that are at the heart of a gang. When I was alone, I would whisper, "I don't want this! I just want to go back!" Through the lens of Louis' illness, I was at last seeing clearly, and I became disillusioned with the drugs, immorality, violence, and aimlessness of gang life. I finally realized that although worldly goods brought pleasure, they brought no lasting joy; and ever so slowly, my conscience, carefully formed by my mom and Father Rosa years before, prodded me to get out. For a long time I tried to hand over the gang to other members. Finally after a year or so, I found someone who agreed to become the head of the Spanish Cobras.

But I would not escape without one final battle. I kept my plans quiet until the change in leadership could be secured. But meanwhile, a rival gang, the Latin Kings, planned to eliminate me, the head of the Cobras, in order to increase their stature in the area.

As much as I try to block out the memory of that night, I can still hear the sudden gunfire, the angry shouts, the terrified screams. There had been no expectation of trouble when we went out that night. I was anticipating being free of the burden of command, and for the first time since my brother got sick, my mood was almost carefree. When the crack of the first shot sounded, we scrambled to defend ourselves.

By this time, I was no stranger to street fights and the smell of blood, but there was so much chaos! The wailing of the sirens could not drown out the sound that came from my own throat as I realized much of the blood was my own. Before it was all over, I had been shot nine times. Both my friends and the Kings believed I was dead, and those able to do so fled the scene.

There is nothing like being flat on your back in a hospital bed to bring life into focus. In what I can now see as the clear intervention of the Holy Trinity, I survived those nine bullets. It took more than a year to recover from my wounds, and in that time, I hit rock bottom. Out of desperation and loneliness, I began to pray, and the prayer that came most easily to me from my childhood was the Holy Rosary. Well, when our Blessed Mother gets involved, things happen. Slowly a hunger grew in me for more of that old faith and ritual that I had known when I was young. My heart began to soften, and I actually began to feel at peace. For maybe the first time in my life, I felt joy—real, deep, abiding joy.

Like Saint Ignatius of Loyola, I had a near-death experience, followed by a long recovery, which brought me back to God. During that time, Father Rosa's example and words kept coming back to me. I could hear so clearly his kind, but stern tone rebuking me, "Uzi, you must go to Sunday Mass; it is the most important thing!"

I also spent a lot of time thinking about my mother and how she struggled to care for her two children. Would all her sacrifice and hard work to provide for us, to take us to catechism classes, and to make sure we received the sacraments be in vain? I remembered that no matter how tired she was or what needed to be done, she always—always—made sure we all went to Mass on Sunday. With these powerful examples in mind, I made two important resolutions: to return to the Church and to get completely out of the gang.

THE PRODIGAL SON

Regrettably, the anger lasted much longer. The anger at my father, at the rival gang, and even at my brother who, like my father and my mother, had abandoned me. He had not only abandoned me, but he left me with the albatross of the Spanish Cobras. Strangely enough, getting out of the gang proved to be the easier of my resolutions to fulfill. The leadership passed on as planned, and during the year of my recovery, I was not troubled with the Cobras. The harder task was attempting to free my heart to love God, and to forgive those who had hurt me. The first time returning to confession was difficult, but liberating. After that huge step, it was much easier to persist in my efforts to form new habits, starting with Sunday Mass. It is impossible to meet Jesus each week and not have Him change us. Often just showing up allows grace to flow into our souls, and so it happened for me.

Once again, during this difficult time of rebuilding my life, it was Father Rosa who became my support. In one of our phone calls, he urged me to get a college education. Looking back, it seems the subsequent years, full of the good things of life, flew by: earning my degree, meeting and marrying a wonderful woman, and above all growing in my knowledge and love of Jesus and His Catholic Church. As my life swelled with love, for God and my family, the burning fire of my anger lessened. I decided it was time to make peace with Dad.

I started simply to talk to him. Those first conversations were not easy, but with God's grace, I was moving in the right direction. For one of our meetings, I decided to do something extra special. I knew my father loved the Chicago White Sox, so I got tickets to a ball game. When he agreed to go, I was a little nervous, but as always, God was with us that day. When I managed to snag a third-baseline foul ball, on a spur of the Holy Spirit's inspiration, I handed it to my dad.

He turned to me and said, marveling and humble, "Out of all the times I wanted to take you to a ball game, you take me." He looked at the baseball in his hand. "And you give me a game ball!"

It was a special day—the healing of our relationship really started with that. I knew that God could do anything, but realizing that He works through such everyday events to touch hearts and renew relationships reminded me of how truly involved He is in each of our lives.

In 2011 Dad moved back to Puerto Rico, so our contact was only by phone until my wife and I decided to take a family trip to visit. Relations were much better between us, but there was still some tension, and we hoped this time together would help. When we arrived at Dad's house, I stood outside, hesitating before approaching the door.

"I know things will be different," I told my wife, "here in the country where Dad grew up. I just hope we can finally understand each other."

The time surrounded by extended family was a grace-filled and unique moment in our lives. It was clear that God was at work as Dad and I talked through many things, including why he left my mother. He blamed himself for not being content to settle down with his family and for lacking discipline. As he spoke, I felt all the bitterness and anger of those years come right to the surface, and I burned with shame at my coldness toward my father. I interrupted his flow of memories.

"Dad," I said, "I am so sorry for being a bad son." Simple words, but they had taken me years to say. He sat there quietly for a moment, and then he spoke the words I had never expected to hear.

"Uzi, I am sorry for being a bad father." We did not need to say any more. We stood and embraced, seemingly for hours.

When the conversation resumed, it seemed natural to talk about faith and the reasons Dad had quit going to Mass. He had complete clarity about the poor choices he had made, telling me he felt the many sins he had committed had made him unworthy to come to church. I knew from my own experience that there was so much peace and healing to be found in the Mass.

"Dad, come back to church. God is so merciful and He waits for you," I urged him. Although I knew one conversation wouldn't change his mind, I could tell that having received forgiveness from each other, and the visit itself, had greatly softened my dad's heart. At that point, I needed to entrust my father's salvation to God. And God did not waste any time.

It was only a month after my family returned to Chicago that I received a call from my cousin telling me Dad had passed away. My sadness at this news was eased by learning that Dad had made his confession shortly after our talk and had not missed Sunday Mass until the day he died. I was in awe of the way that God had used my desire for peace with my father to spark the return of his faith. It was my first taste of evangelization.

BEGINNINGS OF EVANGELIZATION

In the time immediately following my father's death, I thought a lot about his return to the Church and I marveled that I had played a small part in that. Reflecting on the grace that had filled my life, I wondered,

"What does it take to get someone to come into or back to the Catholic Church?" I think it is a sign of God being active in our lives that we want to reach out, to help others, and to share His goodness with everyone. In some way, too, being able to share the gospel felt like a way of honoring God, of acknowledging what He had done for me in saving my life.

I decided to begin by getting involved at my parish. I looked into the diaconate, but it didn't seem quite right. There had to be a way to serve right where I was, as a layman, and in a way that no one else could. As I continued to look for what God had in mind for me, I taught marriage preparation classes, and I tried to talk to those around me about Jesus whenever the occasion offered.

I soon realized that being defensive about the Church or expressing too much zeal was not prudent. People will not often be brought to the Church by hearing about fire and brimstone. They want respect, understanding, and love—to be seen and heard as human beings. Only in this context will a sharing of faith have meaning for them. I buried myself in prayer and the sacraments to become better prepared for whatever mission God might have for me. Frequent confession and Holy Communion fed my yearning to help others and bring them to Christ. My family noticed that during this time my gentleness increased, and I more easily expressed my love for them.

Living in Chicago, I often met people who gave me opportunities to show God's love. As my eyes were opened and my heart expanded, I felt a desire to reach out to the outcasts of the city: the homeless, the lonely, and the down and out. Their most immediate need was for food, so I started there. I wanted to make sure that even a sandwich would show God's love, so I made them special.

These were not your basic bologna or peanut-butter-and-jelly sandwiches. In fact, even those to whom I gave the food were surprised at how good they were.

One man exclaimed, "Hey, man, these are nice! This is a really classy sandwich! Thanks. Who should I say thanks to?"

I would always tell those I met, "Thank the Catholic Church, friend." Then I would explain how God loves them and the doors are always open. Sometimes I would even walk with them to the nearest Catholic church and take them inside where they couldn't help but experience the beauty and peace that can be found only in the presence of our Lord.

As with any work of charity, there were bumps in the road. I found that not everyone would take the food. Not everyone was thankful or even kind. But I didn't give up, and I began to reap some fruit little by little, one soul at a time. My own small mission was growing and was teaching me a lot.

As time went on and my family grew, I would often take them with me on my trips to deliver love and sandwiches. What I was doing was so simple, yet so needed, and I wanted our children to see it. Afterward I marveled at how the Holy Spirit worked in our lives to improve our moods, to make us more generous with each other, and to fill us with joy. I clearly felt God leading me to share the gospel on the streets, yet the deeper in I got, the more I felt the need for support, further learning, and a more upfront way to engage others in conversation about the faith.

There were just so many people who did not know God, who had almost no exposure to the truth about their own worth and dignity. Slowly during this period, I came to realize that God was asking me to be His voice to these people. We do not need to wait for someone else to begin the work of evangelization; all of us who know God should be looking for ways to share Him with others right where we are.

ST. PAUL STREET EVANGELIZATION

As with my father's reconciliation with the Church, I saw in my work on the streets that the truest evangelization happens within a relationship. In order to be a good witness to God's mercy and love, I needed to make myself truly open to others. I began to look online for an organization that could help—something that did more than just discuss Church teachings. I knew that the group I was looking for would have the same qualities that had inspired my faith, those Father Rosa and my mother had shown: a deep joy in living a life of faith; the sincere desire to change lives for the better; and a loving, open, merciful approach. I had confidence that God would provide the right direction for my work.

It was not long before I came across St. Paul Street Evangelization. As I learned more about the organization, I felt a growing excitement. The gentle approach, the faithfulness to Church teaching, and above all the intention to meet people right where they are, on the street, searching for God—all this was exactly what I was trying to do myself!

When I connected with Steve Dawson, in one of our first conversations about St. Paul Street Evangelization, he told me, "We want to offer friendship to people, to connect with others and to offer the love of Jesus, not fire and brimstone and condemnation."

"I am with you 100 percent!" I told Steve. I was amazed that he used the exact words that had been running through my head when it came to reaching out to people to share the gospel. Again I was amazed to see the wonders and workings of the Holy Spirit.

To learn more about the organization, I began communicating with the other teams associated with St. Paul Street Evangelization around the world. I learned about the joys and struggles of evangelists in England and Australia and shared many laughs of recognition at the situations and stories they imparted. Wherever people are, the good news can bring healing, joy, and hope. The Church is so universal. I thought to myself, "We are all over the world, but we are all so close with the same heart, the same mind, the same soul." As Saint Paul wrote, "You are all one in Christ Jesus" (Gal 3:28).

Armed with excellent training, plenty of materials, and a sign, I went back to the streets, eager to try out this nonconfrontational approach to evangelization.

JEHOVAH'S WITNESSES

At one point I realized that the Jehovah's Witnesses were very active during certain daytime hours in the neighborhood of Division and Spalding, so I decided I would place the St. Paul Street Evangelization materials where I could witness to the Witnesses. Not only was this location within sight of their building, but it was also just inside the territory of the Latin Kings. This fact made me cautious, but it did not deter me.

Every day that the Jehovah's Witnesses passed my table, we would greet each other. I was always watching for opportunities for deeper conversation, and to offer friendship. I asked questions of the folks passing my corner, and I had the chance then to answer some of their questions about Catholicism. After only one month, the leaders of the Jehovah's Witnesses began to see the danger of such a presence, as their own people were asking them more questions about their teaching. Soon I had one of the leaders of the Witnesses' temple on my corner.

"You need to stop talking to my people," he said to me. "I don't want you saying anything to them or giving them any of your materials."

"With all due respect, sir, I have the right of free speech," I replied. "Your people don't have to stop to talk to me, but if they do want to, then I am allowed to talk to them. I certainly will not approach them in your worship hall, but when they are here on the street, my right to free speech lets me talk to them. Again, with all due respect."

While we were talking, our group was joined by another Witness who, I later learned, was named David. He seemed genuinely interested in what we were saying to each other but did not say anything. The discussion turned into a conversation about our religious differences, and I asked the leader what version of the Bible he used. When he told me, I showed him my Bible.

"Do you know why your Bible is thinner than mine? It's because you have an edited version. Your version contains fewer books because back in the 1500s someone removed a bunch of books that Christians had been using since the time of the apostles. The Catholic Bible has retained all those original books."

As I was saying this, I remained calm and did not raise my voice. Still, I could tell he felt that I was challenging him, and he responded by threatening me. I wanted to remain firm but still open to dialogue, so I did not back down or push back. Where once I would have wanted to teach this man not to mess with me, here I knew that if I was being tempted to make things escalate, it was really the devil who was behind it. To defeat the devil, you stay with the Catholic Church and you rely on the power of God. I watched the two men walk away as I prayed.

Not long after this incident, David returned secretly to speak with me. "I felt the truth of what you were saying," he confided. However, the young man feared the reprisals of his family if he pursued an investigation of the teachings of the Church.

I didn't push David but began through the weeks ahead to explain that our pilgrimage here on earth was but a prelude to life in eternity. My efforts to display kindness and patience resulted in an exchange of phone numbers. I urged him, "Go to a Catholic church and see if you like it."

Weeks went by as we continued to meet and discuss the differences between the Jehovah's Witnesses and the Catholic Church. For six months our conversations continued and sometimes got heated when the doctrines clearly conflicted, but David always came back.

I took him through some of the Bible, showing him the discrepancies in the Jehovah's Witness bible. When David learned that the Catholic Bible had been carefully and prayerfully confirmed in several councils of bishops starting in the first few centuries of the Church, it caused him to examine his beliefs seriously. If the Bible from which he had received his teaching was missing essential parts, what else might he be missing?

From there we discussed the Mass, with its roots in Scripture and Jewish tradition. When I invited David to attend Mass, he fell in love with the liturgy. He began to follow the readings and go to Eucharistic Adoration, but still had not made the break from the Jehovah's Witnesses. Then one day, I received the call I had been praying for. David told me, "I have joined the Rite of Christian Initiation. I have decided to become Catholic!" Thank you, Jesus! A bonus was that David's Catholic uncle was going to sponsor his journey into the Church. From my own life, I knew it would be important that this decision involved someone from his own family.

As David went through the Rite of Christian Initiation of Adults (RCIA), his father remained in the fold of the Jehovah's Witnesses. He was very upset at his son's decision and even called and threatened me several times. "I am going to come after you with a baseball bat for what you are doing!" he shouted at me.

"Sir," I calmly replied, "if you hit me with a bat, I would count it an honor." I knew that this persecution was a sign that I was getting the devil upset with my efforts, yet I had no fear, because I trusted that Mary and Jesus would take care of me.

At the Easter Vigil David came home to the Catholic Church with his uncle at his side. Amazingly, the Holy Spirit began to work not only in David but on his father as well. By the time of the Easter Vigil, David's father had softened to the extent that he actually attended the Mass to witness his son become a Catholic. Even though his mother did not come to the baptism, she had already ceased attending the services of the Jehovah's Witnesses. With David's courage and determination to find the truth, God was pouring out blessings on his family. And with these early successes, God was preparing me to take on something much more challenging. It is proof of how mighty He is that my next big encounter did not send me back to the hospital.

THE LATIN KINGS

Remember that I would set up my table just inside the territory of the Latin Kings. I knew these men and women were hungry for more than what they had, and in spite of my past, I felt confident that with God's grace and our Lady's protection, I could offer them the truth that all hearts long for.

Today the Latin Kings are known as one of the largest and the most violent gangs in the country, with their largest numbers taken from the Latino population of Chicago. The irony is that most of them are baptized Catholics, yet they run drugs and have been found guilty of many crimes from petty theft to murder.

From my past, I knew gangs and how to interact with them. The rules are simple, yet hard to master in the face of fear and intimidation. Don't show any weakness. Speak their language or they will tune out.

There is no use pretending that I did not have some fear of engaging the Latin Kings. After all, they had shot me nine times. But the fear was a physical, natural fear. In contrast, I had no spiritual fear because God is stronger than the devil. Momma Mary would take care of me as she had before in the power of the Holy Trinity.

One afternoon, from my SPSE set-up on the corner of Division and Spalding, I watched them approach—a couple of young toughs. They stopped square in front of my table and looked me and my materials up and down, scorn punctuating their every motion.

"We don't need you! We're members of the biggest gang in the whole country!" one of them sneered. Then they flashed their sign to me.

"Oh, yeah? I belong to the biggest gang in the whole *world!*"

This got them thinking. "What gang is that?" they wanted to know.

I flashed the sign of my gang. I made the Sign of the Cross.

"The Catholic Church!" I replied. They knew the sign since they had been baptized Catholic, but like so many in the inner city, they had fallen away from the practice of their childhood. That afternoon we talked. To my surprise, they stuck around and listened as I talked about the Lord's great mercy. They listened as I told them that Mother Mary's protection is better than any to be found in a gang. In wonder, I listened as they articulated their questions about who Jesus is.

Why should I have been surprised? Wasn't this all the Holy Spirit's work? Aren't gang members just as much God's children as anyone else? And hadn't I once been in their shoes?

They agreed to go to church with me that evening. Not only did they voluntarily enter the building, but they willingly went to confession and attended Mass. I channeled my amazement into praise and thanksgiving to Almighty God. Again, why should I have been amazed? It was Divine Mercy Sunday.

As I continued to talk with these and a few other gang members and began to build trust with them, I knew it was only a matter of time before the leaders got wind of my presence in their territory. Sure enough, before too long I received a demand for a meeting to discuss the "situation". I knew that they would try to intimidate me into leaving their territory, but I was determined to stay strong. I would allow God to speak the truth through me to the most influential gang leaders in my area. Still, I was cautious. Before I left for my destination, I called Steve Dawson.

"Steve, do you have a pen and paper?" I asked.

"Sure. What's up?"

"Here. Write down this address," I said. "If you don't hear from me again, you know that this place is my last known location. I am going to meet the leaders of the Latin Kings."

As I expected, the head of the Latin Kings threatened me as the Jehovah's Witness leader had. But there was a further complication. See, a video of my conversation with some Kings had made it to the Internet, and the gang knew the police would then be able to track down some of them. I understood where they were coming from and agreed to remove the video.

However, I stood firm in the face of their next demand. They wanted me to stop coming to their territory. I was prepared, and I recognized the tactics intended by the devil to strike fear into my heart. Through the entire conversation, as tense as it was, I felt Mary's mantle draped around me, and I was able to counter each demand.

"So you want me to pay you money for protection? That is not going to happen." When they tried to threaten me with physical violence, I calmly answered them, "Do you really want to wake a sleeping giant? Do you want me to go to the pastor, or the bishop?" In bringing up the bishop, I was hoping to appeal to the last bit of respect I knew they held for the Church of their childhood, the Church that buries their dead and comforts their grieving families. Even these tough men recognized that, in the violence that filled their lives, the Church and her leaders are often the only comforting presence in times of crisis. Plus, because of the recent breakup of some of their drug rings with many gang members ending up in prison, the gangs are now more vulnerable. I knew these leaders would recoil at any suggestion of involving authority.

I am convinced that the Blessed Mother made it possible for us to reach a compromise that day. I agreed to move out of their territory, but to continue my work in the same neighborhood. They accepted this and didn't know till much later that all I had to do was move my table across the street. From here, I continue to reach out to everyone who crosses my path. I do not fear the gangs, but I also exercise prudence. The Holy Spirit is still working miracles every day.

GOING FORWARD

The gentle, inviting approach of St. Paul Street Evangelization is a perfect way for Catholics who are uncertain about their ability to share their faith to begin doing so. Evangelization teams have at least two people so that there is support and help on the spot. Still, the most powerful tools of evangelization for any Catholic, wherever they may be, are prayer and the sacraments. I don't recommend to anyone that they go out on the streets unless they are committed to prayer and the sacraments.

When I reflect on my work as an evangelist, one thing stands out to me. The Eucharist truly is our biggest asset. So many times now, I have seen people simply experience Adoration or attend a Catholic Mass for the first time, and realize how much of what they seek is there in the Catholic Church.

There are plenty of spiritually hungry people with broken hearts and homes that could use a friend. For some, it might take as much boldness and courage to visit the sick, the shut-ins, and the lonely in their community as it would to encounter gang members. All need God, and all can be reached by His grace.

St. Paul Street Evangelization has helped me continue on my path to serve God by serving others. Not all people will stop to talk. There are many more who refuse a Rosary than accept it. But it is all worth it for the one or two or three who come home to the Church. I would rather sit at the table all day and reach only one or two out of the hundreds who walk by, than risk the chance that a hungry soul could not find someone who cared enough to bring him the truth. The gift of the Holy Spirit—pure unadulterated joy—is the reward. That is payment enough for the work that we do as street evangelists.

Chapter 5

God's "Second Choice"

Lucy Stamm

Boise, Idaho

The man made direct eye contact as he strode across the small park toward our Rosary-laden picnic table. This was unusual. Usually, we had to entice people near our table with an offer of "free Rosary" or, perhaps, of a brochure about it and its connection to the Bible. But this was a man on a mission.

I tried to prepare myself for anything. My fellow evangelist that Sunday, Nick Roberts, wouldn't be able to help me. He was deeply engaged on the other side of the table in a lively discussion on just how much we can know about the existence of God. Therefore, the approaching conversation was going to have to be one-on-one.

When the man was close enough to hear, I asked, "Would you like a free Rosary?" I figured I might as well stick with what I knew best.

He ignored the Rosaries. "I have a question for you," he countered. "How long have you been a Catholic?"

"Since I was six weeks old," I answered, without batting an eye.

He was the one who blinked.

I wondered to myself, was this one of our "separated brethren from the Reformation" who had a problem with infant baptism? I continued my story. "I was raised Catholic by good Catholic parents and was confirmed when I was twelve years old." By his lack of response to this, I guessed that he was not Catholic himself.

"The Catholic Church teaches that conversion is an ongoing process, rather than a one-time event," I offered. "I have had several conversion experiences in my life. For example, when I was a sophomore in high school, I attended an André Kole show sponsored by Campus Crusade for Christ. That was a time I publicly committed my life to Jesus Christ as my Lord and Savior."

He gave a brief nod. Aha! So, he probably *was* from some non-Catholic Christian background. The more I know about someone's faith background, the better I can adjust my wording so that we can feel as if we're standing on common ground. I want each person that God draws toward us to feel attracted to the Catholic Church, founded by Jesus Christ Himself, and to the inexhaustible treasury of grace that he can find here. Without any language or concepts in common, though, that would be quite difficult.

I continued, "What happened at the show was that I simply ratified the decision already made on my behalf by my parents and godparents at my baptism. I consciously deepened my commitment to Christ that day."

"Have you ever left the Church?" he challenged.

Not my favorite topic. "I've never left the Catholic Church for another faith," I said. "But there was a time when some choices I was making made it too uncomfortable for me to go to Mass for a while. But then God, in His mercy, granted me the grace of repentance and I returned. But I was always Catholic in my heart."

"By 'choices'," he asked, "do you mean the usual dumb teenager stuff?"

"Yes, that's a good way of putting it," I answered. And, yes, only the pure grace of God brought me back—the grace in my daughter's baptism, to be exact.

In Scripture, Jesus warns, "Truly, truly, I say to you, every one who commits sin is a slave to sin" (Jn 8:34). My "dumb teenager stuff", unfortunately, had continued for years past high school. And it had gotten dumber, and darker, until it had me tightly entrapped. But during most of those years, I continued to fight against it. I clung closely to the Church and to the sacraments, especially to the sacrament of reconciliation, and therefore I still had a good measure of freedom and functionality in my life. But then came a day when I felt offended by someone at the parish. And that gave me the excuse I had been secretly hoping for just to stop the struggle, leave the Church, and give in to sin for a while. I walked away.

Was it for two months, or for two years? I don't know. Even at the time, I couldn't answer that question. But I do know that my life took such a serious turn for the worse that most of my energy went toward simply surviving from day to day. Then I made the decision to have my daughter baptized when she was five months old.

However, the only reason I brought my daughter into the Church at that time was cultural. I simply wanted her to be baptized in the same outfit that my sisters and I had each worn on our baptismal days. Yet, because of my discomfort with the Church, I had kept putting it off. But now, if I waited even a month longer, it would be too late—she would have outgrown the vintage family baptismal gown. I didn't have even as unworthy a motive as superstition to have her baptized that day—I was just too dead spiritually to even think about the bigger questions, such as salvation and eternal destiny and life-altering grace. But God was there. And for Him this wasn't an empty show.

I remember being so concerned about appearances that Sunday afternoon. "What will everybody think?" "Is my baby crying too much?" "Is my mother's dementia making me look bad?" I was also acutely aware of where my hired (non-Catholic) videographer was standing and hoping he was getting all the camera angles just right.

Then came the moment of the actual pouring of the water over my daughter's head and the invocation of the triune Name. At that moment, something inside me healed. Suddenly, my heart experienced an unshakeable sense of belonging. With surprise, I realized that I was among my own people. This was quickly followed by the thoughts, "Heavens, where have I been?" and "I need to get to confession!" Then the ceremony was over.

God is faithful. And He is as good as His Word. Just as He warns about becoming enslaved to sin, He immediately follows the warning with a promise, "If the Son makes you free, you will be free indeed" (Jn 8:36). And for the six days following my daughter's baptism, I prepared myself to receive the sacrament of reconciliation. Then, on that next Saturday, I joined the line of penitents waiting in the back of my neighborhood Catholic church.

Soon enough, it was my turn to enter the reconciliation room. Although I felt nervous and ashamed, I confessed my sins out loud to the priest—honestly, yet concisely. Then, knowing that condemnation was what I deserved, I felt thankful when what I received instead, through the ministry of the Church, was absolution from my sins, pardon, and peace. I was now back in full communion with the Catholic

Church. Mass began within the hour, and I couldn't wait to experience the joy of receiving the Blessed Sacrament in Holy Communion once again.

Whenever I look back, I am still surprised that God took my pitiful, blind, going-through-the-motions act of having my daughter baptized, and not only did He grant my daughter new life in the Spirit (making her a new creation fit for eternal life with Him in His Kingdom forever), but He also granted me the unasked-for and unsought gift (the need for which I was completely unaware of at that time) of repentance and (please, God?) lasting conversion.

To this day, I am also awestruck by the raw power and love that God makes available in each of the seven sacraments—not just for the recipients, but also for everyone near. And I know that I have only the tiniest inkling of just how much power and how much love is there. God is so worthy of worship—and so good!

But I didn't tell the man in the park any of this. I probably guessed that he wasn't interested in a discussion on sacramental-grace theology at that moment. What he seemed interested in was hearing about why I am still Catholic.

"So then I actively started attending Mass again," I told him. "But I always felt nervous about discussing the faith with nonbelievers because, although I believed *what* the Church taught, I had no feel at that time for *why* she taught it. So, another major milestone in my faith journey was when the new *Catechism of the Catholic Church* came out in English. As I read the *Catechism*, I absolutely fell in love with the Catholic Church.

"Not only did she have reasons for everything she taught, and solid reasons at that, but they were presented so beautifully, in such a coherent whole, that I couldn't help but draw close in wonder and joy." It was a poet's argument, the argument from beauty. The reasons behind the teachings had already existed and had been well documented for centuries—I just hadn't "seen" it before. "So the advent of the English *Catechism* was another point of conversion for me."

At that, the man seemed content and so he revealed his agenda to me. Evidently, he saw himself as some kind of cult-buster. He wanted to make sure that people had asked serious questions about their faith, whatever it was. He still didn't take a Rosary or any of the Catholic literature or even reveal his own faith affiliation to me.

SECOND CHOICE

So, although I think the man left satisfied, I felt quite frustrated. I hadn't interested him in anything Catholic. I wondered again why God called me to Catholic street evangelization. I seemed so ill-suited for it. Then, as I often do in moments like that, I thought again about one of my Christian heroes from a hundred years earlier—Gladys Aylward.

Gladys was simply a shop girl in England when she read a magazine article about the desperate need in China for Christian missionaries. She tried in vain to convince qualified people to go, but each one turned her down. Finally, her brother challenged her, "Why don't you go yourself?" But the big-name mission society immediately turned her away. After all, she was poorly educated, had no money, didn't speak Chinese, and wasn't even married. It's said that Gladys went home, emptied her purse onto her bed (it had contained two whole pence), and prayed, "Oh, God. Here's my two cents. Here's me. Use me."

At last, she found a smaller mission board who told her, "We do have another missionary in China who would like someone to work with her. If you can get yourself over there, you can have the spot." With much difficulty, she did eventually arrive in the isolated frontier town in upper Mongolia. She ended up serving the Chinese people for many years, with God working through her to turn hearts to Jesus Christ. Decades later, she deflected praise, saying, "I wasn't God's first choice. I don't know who he was or why he didn't go, but he didn't go. So then God asked me."

A NEW TOOL

I take comfort in Gladys Aylward's story every time I'm confronted with my own lack of talent for evangelization, and God knows just how bad I am at this. This is why our backup prayer-support team is so crucial for our street efforts. After all, God is the One who changes hearts and opens eyes, not any clever conversation or argumentation techniques of our own. Consider, for example, the first day I took St. Paul Street Evangelization's "Good News" pamphlets out on the street.

Now *this* was the pamphlet I had been waiting for! Newman Center chaplain and evangelist Father Simon Lobo, CC, had just developed it for us. Hot off the press, the pamphlet addressed questions that had been burning in my heart every day that I had been attempting Catholic street evangelization: how to present the astonishing news about Jesus Christ to nonbelievers—who He really is, what He accomplished, what difference He makes in lives today. How do you present that to someone who has honestly never heard it before? How do you walk someone from clueless to committed Christian in one sitting? Is that even possible?

As soon as I put my small stack of the one-page "Good News" pamphlets out on our table, a married couple stopped by. Ignoring all of the other literature, they asked for a copy of that particular pamphlet. "We're converts and active Catholics," they told us. "We just want to see how the Catholic Church presents this."

As they walked away, I thought to myself, "That was a good sign."

Immediately after this, a man—probably in his late twenties—approached our table. (We found out later that his name was Matt.) He told us that he was "spiritual" but had never belonged to any religion. We kept him engaged in conversation long enough for him to accept a Rosary and a Miraculous Medal. Then I remembered the new "Good News" pamphlet and offered him one as a "good introduction to what Christians believe."

I was surprised when he opened it up and started to read right away. (Most people, if they do accept a pamphlet, just stuff it into a pocket or bag. I can only hope that they look at it later.) Then Matt turned and sat down. I sat down with him to see if he wanted me to tell him the contents, but he didn't respond. Evidently, he had already tuned out the rest of the world and was focused entirely on the pamphlet. Since I was quite familiar with its contents, and since Matt was going through it so carefully, I could easily follow his progress. At a couple of places, the author says, "Now stop and think about this." And Matt did pause and gaze into the distance for a while at each of these points.

Then, when he got to the place of the prayer of commitment to Jesus Christ as Savior and Lord, Matt ducked his head and became quite still for some time. Afterward, he finished the body of the pamphlet. All of this he had done in complete silence, with no prompting from us. (Meanwhile, the team had kept handing out Rosaries and talking with other people.)

Once it was clear that Matt had finished reading and was ready to talk, I sat down with him again. I wanted to know something about him, so I asked for his story.

It turns out that he became stranded in Boise a few days earlier when the plans that brought him here from Boston backfired. So I made sure he had a safe place to stay and a way to connect with employment resources come Monday. Then, reassured that his immediate material needs were covered, I checked to see what questions the pamphlet might have raised for him. "Where is the nearest Catholic church?" was all he asked. There was one only a few blocks away, so I gave him directions and told him that he could attend Mass there that evening.

Since that seemed to be the only question he had, I tried to give him something that wasn't already in the pamphlet. I told him that one of the unique things about the Catholic faith is how Jesus Christ is truly, substantially present in the Eucharist, how the Blessed Sacrament is reserved in the tabernacle, and how people are welcome to go in and pray any time the church building is open. I also mentioned that some people can sense His presence, but most people at least feel a sense of peace there. He immediately stood up and said that was where he was heading.

"But," I cried after him, "it may be locked!"

"Then I'll just wait," he called back. And he was gone. He had taken with him not only the Rosary and medal, but also a Catholic Bible and our "Good News" and "Becoming Catholic" tracts.

Can you imagine? For the first time, you hear the good news about Jesus Christ. You find out that He is as alive today as He was on the day of the Resurrection, two thousand years ago. You find out that He loves you and has been waiting to save you from your sins. You ask Him to do just that and believe that He has begun a new work in your life. And then you find out that He is actually present only a few blocks away! Can you imagine your excitement? Wouldn't you run, too?

Now, clearly the Holy Spirit was at work in this encounter with Matt. The Holy Spirit was the One who helped Father Lobo write the "Good News" pamphlet. He prepared Matt's heart to receive it, gave him eyes to see and ears to hear (cf. Mt 13:16), and opened his heart to understand it. And He orchestrated that whole, long chain of events that brought Matt all the way from Boston to our table at just that hour when we introduced the pamphlet.

True, it helped that we were faithful and were out there that Sunday, as every Sunday. True, it helped that I took along a stack of the "Good News" pamphlets. It helped that I finally remembered to offer one of them to Matt. But it was God who did the converting. My role was to witness the power of God at work in this one, priceless, human soul. And that's no small thing.

CALLED? *ME*?

So, even though I often feel that, like Gladys Aylward, I am a most unlikely candidate for Catholic street evangelization, I continually try to do my part. I've learned to trust that God can, and does, work through anyone who tries to follow His call.

People, though, often wonder why I attempt this, since I'm so painfully shy by nature. After all, I'm blessed with neither good looks nor a winning personality. My conversational skills are generally rough at best, to put it kindly. Indeed, people have actually told me that these are all signs precisely that I am *not* called to be an evangelist, and that therefore I should just relax and leave that job to someone else.

So why do I keep hanging onto the idea of serving God as an evangelist? Why don't I just let go of that dream? It used to be a difficult question for me to answer. For more than forty years, there was absolutely no external confirmation that this was God's will for me. There was only a persistent, internal sense of being called to evangelize, to bring people into the Catholic Church, to get them to see what a treasure trove of grace she has for them here. I wanted them to want the joy of becoming a saint.

I remember trying to talk out loud in class in high school about Jesus Christ. I remember trying to argue with my non-Christian college roommates. I remember trying to talk about the faith with fallen-away family members, with people in line in grocery stores, with friends who were nonbelievers. And, although a few agreed to attend Mass with me a time or two, no one showed a sustained interest in becoming an active Catholic.

So, through the years, I kept studying. I told myself, "Perhaps if I just know the faith better, I can convince them to come in." Then, "If I know salesmanship, that'll work." Or, "If I understand logic and philosophy and can argue well, then they will come."

The fact that I experienced no success, despite all of this effort, was possibly due to a combination of two main factors. First, I grew up in a home where both of my parents were probably somewhere on the autism spectrum—and therefore I learned few social skills. And second, once I was in college and in an atmosphere where I could learn those skills, I fell prey to a chronic illness that—though invisible—robbed me of most of my ability to concentrate. It made schoolwork difficult, and it made following something as dynamic as a live conversation nearly impossible.

Because of this, I think I struck most people as autistic at best or, perhaps, even mentally ill. Expert opinion, though, from medical and mental-health professionals alike, said that this wasn't the case, that my challenges were due instead merely to the physical illness. And there was evidence that they were correct. On a "good day", I didn't have any problem interacting with people. In fact, people meeting me on such a day often characterized me as "delightful". Unfortunately, those moments were all too rare.

Through it all, I still tried to win people to the faith. Sometimes, I would ask for advice about a specific situation. I would go to a priest or a deacon and say, "Hey, I'm working with someone who has this problem with the Catholic Church. What can I say to help heal the wound and help him get past that?" Invariably, I would get this response: "Lucy, please don't say anything about it yourself! Just have them come in and talk to me." And, of course, I never persuaded anyone to do even that much.

And that undermined what little confidence I had left. I got more and more tongue-tied. By this time, if someone asked me *what* the Catholic Church taught on any particular topic, I could answer immediately, lucidly, and in as much detail as anyone could possibly want. Arguing effectively, though, remained completely beyond my ability. I could not lead people from where they were to where I knew true happiness awaited. So the question remained, why did I still desire to be an evangelist? Why wasn't I content just to teach classes at my parish?

The truth was, these "logical" solutions were contradicted deep inside my soul by a nagging, recurrent sense that my duty lay in active evangelization. This doesn't mean that I didn't try to find other ministries. I did, but there was no peace. Then came one day, no different from any other day. To that point, I had racked up more than thirty years of failure at attempts to evangelize, attempts that admittedly were occurring farther and farther apart. On this particular day, I experienced a brief mystical encounter.

During the experience, the only words exchanged were ... about evangelization. Suddenly, I felt the need to apologize for not fulfilling Jesus' Great Commission, "Go therefore and make disciples of all nations" (Mt 28:19). But I immediately followed the apology with an excuse, "But I'm really bad at it." The response was, "Don't you think I know that?" Then the sense of the loving Divine Presence faded. What remained, though, was an inner wellspring of courage—in addition to that persistent, interior conviction of being called to evangelize.

VOCATION SEARCH

Another few years followed, during which I deepened my prayer life and broadened my understanding of the Catholic faith. Still, though, I wasn't evangelizing. By this time, "The New Evangelization" had become a buzzword in the Catholic Church. My parish even formed an Evangelization Committee—which I immediately joined. Newly formed, though, it was in the study/planning mode and still far from putting a program into action. Since it also didn't work well with my schedule, I dropped out after only a few months.

A bit later, I joined the vocations-discernment group at the local college's Newman Center. I was the token "old person" in a room full of college freshmen and sophomores. It meant a lot to me to be able to attend the meetings. I knew I wasn't "vocations material" in any traditional sense, but I had this burning desire to serve God and it still refused to let up.

Then, on the last Sunday of September 2012, as the vocations group was breaking up after its monthly meeting, I overheard one of the freshmen say to another, "I'm heading downtown to meet Morgan for Catholic street evangelization." There was no way I was going to miss this! I invited myself along.

When I got downtown, I met Ross Hoffman, who had brought St. Paul Street Evangelization to Boise only a week or so earlier. And sitting with Ross was Val Allen, the woman who had chaired the Evangelization Committee at my parish! She had heard about SPSE on Facebook. By the time I found them that day, they were just getting ready to put things away. So I arranged to meet them out there again the following week.

At first, I knew nothing about SPSE and its unique approach to Catholic street evangelization. My understanding was still locked into the Catholic Evidence Guild model, developed in Great Britain during the early twentieth century: stand up on a platform, make a speech, and then answer any and all objections called out to you by the crowd. But Val and the other members of the Boise team weren't doing anything like that. Instead, I saw them simply offer a free Rosary to people passing close by and then hold a quiet conversation with them if they were interested.

The approach was so different from everything I had read about, that at first I couldn't understand how it could be effective. But as I watched the rest of our team in action, it soon began to make sense. Our goal was to attract people to take a serious look at the Catholic faith. Therefore, we wanted to do everything we could to avoid creating a sense of confrontation and animosity. We wanted instead to set up a nonthreatening forum where people could come to get their concerns respectfully addressed and their questions answered. Offering free Rosaries is effective because, after all, what is more visibly Catholic than a Rosary?

You might think that, after waiting for more than forty years to be able to do active evangelization, I would be out there having the time of my life. Instead, I was out there feeling very frightened. Besides feeling tongue-tied, I had the irrational fear that someone was going to shoot us at any moment. No one did, of course. In fact, in the literally thousands of encounters we've had, even anger has been practically nonexistent. (I credit that, though, to our incredible backup prayer-support team and to God's gracious answers to their prayers!) Still, for more than the first year, I battled waves of fear every single week as I got ready to head downtown.

We continued to meet at the same downtown park during the Sundays of October 2012. I know that during that time I didn't have a significant conversation with anyone about the faith, and I was barely able to get people to accept the free Rosary I offered. I saw my role mostly as one of on-site prayer support. Still, I was experiencing a deep inner certainty that this was something I was meant to be a part of. When I told the director of the vocations-discernment group that I would be missing the rest of the meetings that semester, he said, "Don't worry about it. I think you've found your vocation."

WINTER BREAK

As October drew to a close, our local team's founder, Ross, let us know that he was heading out of the country for his annual extended pilgrimage to Rome and holy places beyond. He said we would start up again in the spring, once the weather got warm. The rest of the group disbanded, but I couldn't let it go. I didn't have a sign, I didn't have any pamphlets, and I didn't have anyone to go with me. But I had to do something, so I kept showing up every Sunday afternoon—rain or shine—to pray the Rosary for the conversion of Boise.

In those days, especially when no public event was taking place, that little downtown park was not, shall we say, a place a family would head to for a picnic. Instead, the only people using the area were on skateboards, their wheels screeching across the cobblestones. The only conversations were the angry obscenities they hurled at one another. Even the city police seemed to avoid the area.

But I showed up on Sunday afternoons and quietly paced back and forth near the area where our table had been, unobtrusively praying the Rosary. And peace descended. Although I never spoke with the skateboarders until much later, the cursing and foul language suddenly ceased. Their conversation also changed until it seemed happier and more normal. I considered that a sign, telling me unmistakably, "You're supposed to be here, doing this. This is making a positive difference."

Encouraged, I continued to show up week after week throughout the Christmas season and into the following January. Somehow, word got back to Ross. So he came out one more time that winter—just long enough to entrust me with the SPSE sign and the team's supply of Rosaries and other materials.

This forced me out of my comfortable background prayer-support role and into actual live evangelization. Fortunately, the winter weather kept the number of passersby to a manageable level. Unfortunately, self-doubt and lack of confidence began a serious attempt to drown out that inner voice that had been calling me to be an evangelist. I was seriously out of my comfort zone. But I gamely showed up anyway.

And this is when the weather "miracles" started to happen. No matter how miserable the weather had been, leading up to Sunday afternoon, it always cleared up and became relatively pleasant during the hour I set up our table.

One week, soon after I was put in charge of the team materials, a rare ice storm came through and left a two-inch layer of ice on everything. Then, immediately following the ice storm, came a temperature inversion that kept everything frozen down into the single digits. For Boise, that was extreme weather, and so almost nobody was venturing outside.

Then came Sunday afternoon. Suddenly, the sun began to shine and the temperature rose to a relatively balmy seventeen degrees. Therefore, I showed up with my sign and the Rosaries. But, of course, the picnic table was covered with a two-inch layer of ice. I started breaking it off with my hands, and then saw something I had not seen in the four months I had been coming to that park—a park employee. And he had a snow shovel! I asked if he would help clear the ice off the table, and he gladly went to it with a will. Soon a second park employee with a snow shovel jumped in, and the two of them had the table clear and dry within just a few minutes.

The table was dry, but my dollar-store stretch-knit gloves were dripping wet from the snow and ice that I had begun to scoop off the table by hand. I thought to myself, "Wet gloves in seventeen degrees? I've got about twenty minutes until frostbite sets in. Today is going to be a *short* session!" I decided I would stay until my hands started to get cold and then I would hurry to the car. No need to be stupid, after all. So, I wrung as much water out of my gloves as I could and then proceeded to lay out the Rosaries and pamphlets. Funny thing was, my hands stayed warm. Not just tolerably warm, but comfortably warm! And they remained warm until our regular closing time, when I noticed a slight chill. Then I did hurry to the car, but my hands never got colder than "slightly cool". I took that as another confirming sign that "God wants us out here, doing this."

The next week, Val Allen was able to join me. She wasn't often available on Sunday afternoons, but she came out when she could. The temperatures in Boise had remained well below freezing, so nothing in the park had visibly changed since the previous week. The table was still clear and dry, so we didn't need to worry about our hands getting wet. But Val worried about standing on the thick layer of ice that still surrounded it. She had worn thin dress boots and was afraid that her feet would be too cold to let her stay. But God blessed us again. When we arrived, the sun came out. It continued to shine so cheerfully that people started venturing outdoors and through the park. Soon, Val was engaging people in conversations about the faith. And, again, both Val and I remained comfortably warm until "closing time".

VAL ALLEN

As always, it was a pure joy for me to watch Val Allen work. She has all the natural gifts for evangelization that I lack. What few skills I have picked up, I have learned from watching her.

She grew up Catholic, raised by good Catholic parents. Like far too many, though, after high school Val drifted away, first from the Mass, and then from the faith. What brought her back, several years later, was seeing a non-Catholic Christian coworker studying the Bible during her breaks and lunch hours. This reawakened in Val her own hunger for God and His Word. It wasn't long before Val sat down to talk with the woman. Her coworker shared a few Scripture verses with her, and they prayed together. Afterward, Val found the nearest Catholic parish and made an appointment with the priest for the sacrament of reconciliation.

Now Val is married to a good man, who also became Catholic. She developed her passion for apologetics and evangelization when some of her family members became involved with people who had decidedly anti-Catholic beliefs. She learned early on that preaching and teaching were ineffective when trying to attract people to the Church. On the other hand, she found it natural and easy simply to engage people in friendly conversation.

"The key thing," Val explained to me, "is to learn where the person currently is in their faith journey. Remember, whatever problem or challenge the person has, the answer is Jesus Christ." And the surest path to Him is through the Church that He established. "So," she said, "I find out what hurdles or misconceptions about the Catholic Church the person is holding onto. Then, with so many resources available for finding the truth—in God's Word and in His Holy Church—it's usually just a matter of pointing them in the right direction."

Although most of the encounters Val has experienced as an evangelist with St. Paul Street Evangelization have been positive, there have been a couple of difficult ones. The most difficult of all happened on one of our earliest outings.

Several years previously, Val had taken a workshop from the Catherine of Siena Institute, which provides Catholic parish-based training in discernment, evangelization, and lay formation. In the workshop, Val learned that if someone says, "I don't believe in God," her reply should be, "Tell me about the God you don't believe in."

"It was a great request", she told me later, "and it has helped me many times." So on this day, she asked a man if he was a Christian, and he replied that he was an atheist. Then she made that perfect request.

"His reaction," she said, "was a toxic stream of every horrid thing written and said about the Catholic Church and any organized religion. There were so many nonfacts, partial facts, and ancient errors that it was obvious that here was a person filled with anger and pain." As he ranted, Val told me, her thoughts kept returning to these words from Scripture, "So faith, hope, love abide, these three; but the greatest of these is love" (1 Cor 13:13).

Remaining patient, Val finally got a chance to ask his name. Then she said, "Wow, Mike, what gives you hope and the resolve to get out of bed in the morning?"

He replied with a description of the profound beauty of God's creation: the crisp blue sky, the evergreens, the sun, the unique people, and so on. Val then led the discussion in the direction of the Big Bang versus Intelligent Design.

She asked, "How does the Big Bang theory explain how a seed from one type of flower creates a flower of the same kind? And, more importantly, how does it explain how a man and woman are able to create offspring with only their DNA?" Mike didn't have a response.

Next, Val asked, "Would it be okay to kill someone if they just made you angry? Or, would it be okay to seek out and have sex with married women?"

He answered, "No, of course not!"

"Why?"

"It is just wrong!" he said.

Val asked him, "Who said so?"

"Everyone just knows that!"

Val responded by telling him that she was happy that he had a moral compass, because that could come only from consideration of a judgment from a greater power. She ended the conversation by telling him how much God loves him and how merciful He is to those who return to Him.

Mike replied, "You need to do better than that," and started to walk away.

When Val told him she would pray for him, he said she shouldn't waste her time. Val replied, "It may well be the most important thing I do." Although she saw him pass through the square again a couple of weeks later, he didn't reengage in conversation. Val still prays for him.

And, certainly, that was a most difficult and patience-straining encounter. It was unusual, though. The following is much more typical.

On a marvelously busy spring day, a twenty-year-old body builder approached our table. On his arms, he was sporting Christian tattoos. When Val commented on them, he said that he felt called to become a pastor. He saw "a need to appeal to young people", he said, and told us his dream of setting up a gym as a church.

True to form, Val checked to see how his relationship with the Catholic Church was. He saw it as positive. "The Catholic Church is the grandparent of all Christian churches," he said. He had even attended some Catholic youth events with a friend. But then came his real objection, "I'm just not willing to change some things in my life."

"What things are those?" Val asked. However, since she had a good guess exactly where his challenge lay, she jumped to the heart of the matter. "Does it have something to do with premarital sex or contraception?"

"Yes," he admitted.

Val then explained that it would be easier for him to work through his issues if he belonged to a community who believed the truth about that and who could help him through it. He agreed and accepted SPSE's "Sexual Purity" and "Contraception and Sterilization" pamphlets.

By the time the body builder took his leave from Val, he was open to learning more about the Catholic faith. In parting, he also gladly accepted a copy of the *Catechism of the Catholic Church*.

GROWING THE TEAM

Val Allen is also good at encouraging people to join us and try their hand at evangelization. One of the things that has helped is that the Boise team has established a regular time and place where they practice the ministry. Although they sometimes go out at other times and to other places, Val knows that if she sends someone to the downtown park between 2:00 and 3:00 P.M. on any Sunday afternoon, he will find us.

This comes in handy because she does a lot of her recruiting during the coffee hour following the Sunday morning Masses. Since she knows the team will always be there, she doesn't worry about coordinating around her own hectic schedule. Besides, sometimes it takes an extra week or two for a person to work up the courage to come out the first time. (That irrational fear of being gunned down by an unseen sniper seems to be a favorite ploy of the enemy to keep evangelists off the street. I've heard more than one person mention it.)

But Val doesn't limit her recruiting ability to safe church circles. Consider what happened on another day when only the two of us were working together.

A man named Joseph approached close enough to our table to hear me offer him a free Rosary. "No," he said, because he wasn't Catholic anymore.

Val kept the conversation going, "Do you mind my asking what happened? What drew you away?"

And so Joseph kept talking. And as he talked, he started saying that at least he admired the Catholic Church for this or for that. And then he started saying that it was a shame and that it was so unfair that the Catholic Church was being attacked because of this or because of that. And then he started saying how the Catholic Church's teaching was so much more solid and biblically based on this point and on that point than the teachings of this or that other religion that he had joined.

(Of course, it probably helped that, whenever he disagreed with what another group believed, Val or I would agree with him and confirm his healthier interpretation with a quotation from the Bible or from Church teaching. And each time, he would respond with, "Yes, that's right", before going on. And our doing this probably simply reminded Joseph of what he had learned years ago, back in Catholic grade school, but had since forgotten. Nothing new, nothing novel—just good, solid Catholic teaching.)

Then came the moment when Joseph laid out for us his spiritual journey. I'll spare you all the details, but it began "I was raised Catholic" and it ended "and now I've come full circle back to the Catholic Church." The conversation had lasted about forty minutes.

We made sure that he chose a local parish and received the contact information for their "Returning Catholics" program. Val then said, "You know the faith so well, you should join us."

He glanced at his watch and replied, "Well, I've got a few minutes to spare. Okay."

Immediately, another man approached our table. Shawn. Talking about our Lady, he was smiling, but difficult to understand. So he spelled it out for us. It wasn't flattering.

But praise God for our backup prayer support! Val took the lead in her lovely, maternal way and calmly insisted that purity was an essential part of Mary's being the Mother of God.

Shawn countered with Mary's stated need for a Savior.

"Yes, Mary needed a Savior," Val explained. "And she was saved at the moment of her conception." And so the conversation went.

Meanwhile, I simply stepped back and played the supporting role. I handed Shawn pamphlets as the conversation prompted (and he accepted them all), prayed when outbursts of rage seemed imminent from admittedly inebriated Shawn, and worked at keeping newly returned-Catholic (and now novice-evangelist) Joseph calm.

By the grace of God and Val's conversational skills, the initial crisis soon passed, and Shawn progressed from trying to insult our Lady to bemoaning his troubles with alcohol. Here, Joseph stepped forward and spoke to Shawn man-to-man as only an older man can to a younger one, and with the moral authority of one who has wrestled with self-indulgence and overcome it.

When the conversation moved on to the topic of work, it turned out that Shawn and Joseph both practiced the same trade—welding. So, not only was Shawn unable to get away with any self-pitying excuses, but Joseph was also able to direct him to a worksite that was hiring. It was a joy to watch.

Finally, Val sensed that the moment had come. She asked Shawn's permission for us to pray for him. At first, he was taken aback, but then he consented. Val laid a gentle hand on his arm and asked the Holy Spirit to grant Shawn deliverance and guidance and openness to God in his life. The rest of us gave a resounding "Amen!" including Joseph.

Val told me later, "One of the things I like most is praying for people." She said, "Some I pray for in the moment, and some I add by name to my daily prayer."

"READY FOR HARVEST"

Val's casual mention of "daily prayer" is especially telling. I, too, have found that commitment to prayer and spiritual growth are keys to effective evangelization. That is because, ultimately, evangelization is God's work!

I've seen His hand out here so often now, in my first two years on the team, that it has become much easier to ignore those Sunday-morning whiffs of fear when they try to reappear. And, once I started having return visits from people I had spoken with months earlier, and heard evidence of conversion miracles, it became easier to believe that our efforts are fruitful—even when we don't get to see the yield.

Still, when a Sunday comes along and I am the only team member available, I feel dismayed. It doesn't keep me home, but one Sunday I was especially disappointed because, on that day, a Catholic high school student and his father would be joining us. The student was an on-fire, aspiring evangelist who was coming along for his first look at real-life Catholic street evangelization. I had so hoped they would be able to see genuine evangelism at work.

Right away, we seemed to have nonstop visitors. The first three people who stopped at the table each told us they only "used to be" Catholic. But each soon had their fears calmed about the sacrament of reconciliation, had been matched to a parish in the area, and had indicated a commitment to return to active practice of the faith. As the third person in a row was walking away, map and brochures in hand, I overheard the dad say to his son, "And it's as easy as that!" Though admittedly still unusual, it was at least evidence that at some point God had turned even me into an actual evangelist.

Indeed, Catholic evangelization is all God's work but, paradoxically, He calls each of us to do our part in it. So, whether you are a "natural" like Val, or a "not God's first choice" like me, God is calling you by name and can work wonders through you. Jesus says, "Lift up your eyes, and see how the fields are already white for harvest" (Jn 4:35). What is He calling you to do about it?

Chapter 6

Oh Beauty, Ever Ancient, Ever New

Ed Graveline

Las Vegas, Nevada

I swung between conscious thought and a dream-like state where the pain of my battered skull barely registered. Just in front of me, the sounds of cursing and a grating of metal on metal went on and on.

"God," I pleaded, "I know I haven't given you much thought these past few years, but I need help now!"

I must have moaned or made some noise because just then a kick to my ribs sent another wave of pain and nausea to drown all consciousness. When I came to, I could see the robbers clustered around the safe just outside the crowded office, arguing over how to move it farther or break it apart where it stood. They had already broken through the door frame and then used the hand truck to try to move the heavy safe out of the small office and out the back into their van. But it had taken all their combined strength to move it just a few yards before they had given up.

"I bet that kid knows the combo; we can make him tell us," one of them insisted. I had already endured almost twenty minutes of their brutal beating, and now at the thought of more, I tensed in fear. Never, in my years, training as a star high school and college athlete, pushing my body to do awesome and impossible feats, had I felt anything like the pain and humiliation of being beaten by these three desperate and angry men.

"No way he knows," one of the other men argued. "We beat the [—] out of him already. He's just whining and crying there. If he knew how to get himself out of this, he would have said so by now."

It was true: if I had known the combination, I would have told them. Instead, on this my first night being trusted to close up the restaurant, my manager had left the safe door open for me, ready for the end of the day. All I had to do, he instructed, was put the cash and receipts in and close the door. We never imagined that anything would go wrong. Yet here I was, big man on campus, star basketball player, the man who didn't need God, begging and pleading, and yes, crying for help of any kind.

I was raised in southern California, the fourth in a family of six children. My parents loved their Catholic faith and did their best to pass it on to each of us, but somewhere in the busy years of high school and early college, I became much more attracted to the excitement and pleasures of the world than to a life of faith. I hadn't consciously rejected my faith; it just didn't fit with my new lifestyle of sex, drugs, and rock and roll. Now, however, as I faced the very real possibility of death, the teachings of my childhood snapped clearly into focus, particularly those about God's hatred of sin.

As the thieves, just a few feet away from me, argued and struggled to get at the money in the safe, I continued my silent and intense dialogue with God. I told Him everything. The years of drinking, smoking pot, missing Mass, using girls, disappointing my parents—everything. He became the most real Person in that room. In a purely human sense, I had never felt so alone and so helpless, and yet in the depths of my soul, I was aware of a profound peace and the unmistakable presence of God. Convinced I was going to die, I made the most sincere act of contrition of my life. Over and over, I prayed the words of repentance learned as a child.

Suddenly, I was recalled to the present by a sharp crack on my head. It was the first man, the one who was ready to keep torturing me. He was demanding that I open the safe, and I knew I had to try once again.

Somehow, I found the strength to stand and stagger to the large, fireproof safe. I knelt down, and spun the dial to the first digit. Silently, and without really looking at my hands, I prayed. *Help me, Jesus.* Another spin. *I'm truly sorry for my sins.* Then the third digit. *Forgive me my sins.* Finally the fourth, *I firmly resolve to amend my life.* I hesitated and grasped the handle. I don't know who was more amazed as the door swung open! *Thank you, Jesus!* I whispered. One terrific blow to my head and I lay quiet.

During the next six days in the hospital, I had plenty of time to reflect on my priorities and to think more deeply about how my life had been miraculously preserved. I found that the words I had prayed so earnestly on the floor in the restaurant remained with me, and a desire to live for God who is "all-good and deserving of all my love" grew stronger the more I thought about what I had gone through. There was no earthly reason why that safe should have opened, or why all the beatings to my head hadn't killed or crippled me. Clearly, God had heard my prayers and decided that I needed more time on this earth. The more I thought it over, the plainer it seemed to me that I needed to make good on my promises to amend my life. And there was a lot that needed changing.

It is said that the greatest miracle God can work is the healing of a heart. Somehow, through the brutal beating I had received, I was healed in the deepest part of my soul. No longer would I be living for myself.

God gave me the extra grace, not only to leave my old life behind, but to dive into a life dedicated to Him. I had two girlfriends at this time, one at home and one at college. I broke up with both of them, then set about removing myself from the crowd of my partying friends. Strangely, it was not hard to make these breaks since most of the relationships were based on immoral activities, not true friendships. Through it all, the sense of God's closeness never left me, and the yearning to know Jesus only grew stronger.

THE WAY, THE TRUTH, AND THE LIFE

A few weeks after I was released from the hospital, I returned to Northern Arizona University where I had a basketball scholarship. Greg, one of my teammates, invited me to join a Bible study held early Wednesday mornings run by an interdenominational group, the Navigators. Since one of the challenges of living my new life would be to show the new me to my teammates, I agreed to go. I also hoped that I would make some new friends, people who were living the kind of life I wanted. I knew many Christians had beliefs that differed from the Catholic teaching I had grown up with, but really, how different could we be? Would it even matter?

That first morning, we began by studying the Gospel passage about the Last Supper. The leader turned to me and said, "Ed, you are Catholic, but when you receive Communion, you don't really believe that you are eating Jesus' Body and drinking His Blood, do you? If you do, you are a cannibal!"

Stunned at such a proclamation that I had never considered before, I sheepishly answered, "I don't know!" I never imagined I would have to defend my newly rediscovered faith while hanging out with other Christians! And how could anyone imagine that the Mass, with its beauty, peace, and ancient ritual, could be connected with something so ugly? That night, I knew what I had to do—call Dad. Before getting married, my father had studied for twelve years to be a Jesuit priest, stopping just before ordination. Surely with his background, he would know how to explain the Eucharist. Being a wise man, he recommended that I go straight to the source and read chapter six of Saint John's Gospel, the discourse on the Bread of Life.

"Does the leader believe in the Trinity?" Dad asked. When I answered that he did, Dad continued, "Does he believe the Trinity is human or divine? If he believes the Trinity is divine, how can he claim we are cannibals when we are consuming what is divine?"

I read and reread chapter six. Eight times I went through that chapter. The last time, when I came to John 6:66: "After this many of his disciples drew back and no longer went about with him", it echoed within me. *No longer went about with him.* Jesus did not chase after the ones who left, reassuring them that He was just speaking figuratively. He let them go, fully aware that they were rejecting His scandalous claim that they must consume His very Body. There was no doubt. I had to go back to the Navigators and tell the leader about this.

At the very next meeting, I brought up the subject he had addressed the week before and told him all about chapter six in Saint John's Gospel. My newfound knowledge and conviction must have made the leader uncomfortable because he asked me to stop coming to the meetings. In God's providence, this Bible study class became a great turning point in my life as I realized: *I need to know my faith.*

That semester, Dad and I had many conversations as he guided my exploration of Church teaching. My hunger for the truth blossomed as I drew from the wells of Catholic literature. The masters of the Catholic life such as Saint Augustine, Saint Teresa of Avila, and Saint John of the Cross helped satisfy the thirst within my soul. *The Baltimore Catechism* helped instruct me in basic Catholic teachings that I had forgotten or ignored. *Catholicism and Fundamentalism* by Karl Keating helped even more. I graduated with my degree, but also with an enriched and enlivened faith.

It was not only the moral teachings of the Church that worked on my heart, but the sheer goodness of the ordinary people I met who quietly tried to live their faith. There is nothing more compelling than seeing goodness in action. God saved my life that day in the restaurant, and at the same time awakened my conscience and my soul so that my life would be worth living. I no longer even had the desire to control my own future but was ready to give all over to Him.

TEACHING THE FAITH

When, some years later, I moved to Las Vegas for work, I looked around for a good source for Catholic books so that I could continue to learn about the Church. I was blessed to find, not only a great book store, but one of those people who quietly and beautifully lived out his faith. Joe, the store owner, and I became good friends over many conversations. Jokingly, we discussed teaching a class to local parishes on Catholic apologetics where we could share our knowledge and passion for our faith. Slowly the joke turned serious, and we became deep in planning.

Although neither of us had a formal background in theology, we shared a solid, self-educated foundation in the faith and a passion and drive to go deeper. We also had the desire to help ordinary folks understand and love their own faith more. Our enthusiasm, motivation, and demonstrable knowledge of Catholicism convinced a couple of pastors to allow us to offer apologetics sessions at their parishes. Soon we were slated to teach a class that would be held at two parishes on alternate months—Saint Peter's Church on the southeast side of Las Vegas and Saint Elizabeth Ann Seton on the northwest side. We had the venues and we had the plans; now we just needed the people.

Imagine my delight and surprise when about seventy-five people attended the first class! The classes continued for several years and eventually relocated to Our Lady of Las Vegas, right in the center of the city. If ever there was a city that needed to be reminded of God's goodness and His amazing plan for mankind, it was Las Vegas. As for me, I could feel the peace of knowing I was doing what God wanted of me, and was putting all my reading, studying, and questioning to good use.

At one point while I was teaching at Our Lady of Las Vegas, a woman raised her hand and asked if she could bring her brother to class. But, she cautioned, he was a Baptist, a strong, anti-Catholic Baptist. Much to my surprise, he came. One of the first claims he made in class was that even babies and those who are severely handicapped were steeped in sin. He looked at me with a challenging air, daring me to find some way of contradicting him. "Well," I began, "I think you probably understand something different than I do when it comes to free will." To my amazement, he sat back and listened to every point as I slowly worked my way through the Church's teaching on original sin and free will. And then, the next week, he came back ... and the next week ... and the next. With growing excitement, I realized that he was finding the teachings of the Church as compelling as I had!

My college experience, in which the Christian Bible study leader had asked me to leave the group rather than have his ideas challenged, was forefront in my mind throughout this time. And another idea was also brewing. If there were other Christians, or even non-Christians, out there who would be willing to engage in a dialogue, to really stop and listen to what the Church has to say, could I be the one to reach out to them? Could we really build on our common ground to come to the truth?

The more I taught apologetics, the clearer I saw the need for cultivating a love for those whom I engaged in discussion. I was learning that the beautiful truths of our faith have to be presented to individuals within the context of their own lives; that is, the real good news of Catholicism is God's love for each of us. I knew that God had come to me, deep in my sinful life, when I was near death that night in the restaurant. He had heard me, forgiven me, and saved me only so that I could live more fully and happily. And very naturally, the more I loved God, the easier it was for me to love and accept all of the teachings of the Church, even those that seem most difficult to worldly minds. And certainly, I had lived the way of the world and I knew its falseness.

Early on, I had come to recognize that any efforts of mine in trying to convince people of the truth of Catholicism were merely to plant the seed and leave the rest to the Holy Spirit. In fact, the Baptist man did continue to study the teachings of the Church, and eventually he became Catholic. The work of the Holy Spirit was powerful in his life, leading him to study at a Byzantine seminary and be ordained a priest.

Today, Father Diodoro Mendoza is known all around our area for his holiness and orthodoxy.

Our Bible studies and apologetics classes continued to be well attended, pushing both Joe and me to continue to learn, to be informed about the issues of the day, and to find new ways to present the information. As time went on, I became more and more interested in politics and the practical ways that our faith can impact the world around us.

During the 2012 election year, I organized a Catholic voters' guide and worked hard on informing Catholic voters of the stances of various candidates running for office. As a result of this work, I no longer taught the Bible study classes. It seemed that once again God was pointing me in a new direction.

At this time, I would occasionally visit some websites where people could debate questions of faith. It was on one of these sites that I first saw the link to St. Paul Street Evangelization and from there began to explore their work. Although I had never tried to engage people on the street to discuss faith, I was itching to get back to teaching, and I had a strong desire to share my own experience of faith as well. I decided to learn more about this unique approach to evangelization.

After talking with Steve Dawson on the phone, I was eager to begin a chapter in Las Vegas. He sent me the materials, and by the middle of January 2013, I had gathered several other volunteers. Sunset Park, where we decided to begin our adventure in street evangelization, is situated on a lake fringed with trees, a peaceful setting very conducive to our work. On the first outing we spent two and a half hours at the park resulting in ten or fifteen contacts. Some were Baptists and some were Mormons and others were fallen-away Catholics. Those we spoke to seemed interested and curious about our nonconfrontational approach and our unusual mission. "No, all our materials are free," I repeated. "We just want to give you a chance to know Jesus and know what the Catholic Church is really all about." It was exhilarating taking such a bold step!

While we were happy to have connected with the people at the park, it became apparent that we could reach many more people if we went to the Las Vegas Strip, a four-mile stretch of South Las Vegas Boulevard, dense with casinos and ritzy hotels. We first set up in front of the Encore Hotel, but the management did not want us there. Not wanting to gain a reputation as troublemakers, we decided to move to another location farther down the Strip.

This time, we set up near the Mirage Hotel and Casino. As long as we did not obstruct the sidewalk or bother the people walking by, the management had no complaints. Mike, who came on those first missions and continues to be one of our strongest evangelists, often comments that Vegas is called Sin City for a reason. There are so many troubled souls walking by! Many people pass without taking a second glance in our direction; however, the encounters we have had are nothing short of marvelous.

TEAM WORK

Mike and I have been working together for over a year now. We have found that we each have gifts that complement the other. Because of my history of teaching apologetics and Bible studies, I can address doctrinal questions and quote sacred Scripture to support the teachings of the Church. Mike, on other hand, readily admits that he refers such questions to me because his focus is on the Divine Mercy. We always bring images of Jesus as the Divine Mercy and literature explaining the devotion when we evangelize on the Strip. As I learned when we first started teaching Bible study classes, it is not enough just to tell people about the doctrines of the Church. Doctrines matter very little to those who don't even know the Lord. By far the greatest work we do on the street is simply to listen, to pray with people who stop, and to tell them about God's love and mercy.

One of the best examples of how sharing God's mercy can open a heart to hear the truth occurred when Mike spoke with a young woman who worked in Las Vegas. At first, she seemed reluctant to stop at our table. Was it because there was a picture of Jesus staring right at her and she was rather scantily clad? Who knows? Nevertheless, Mike asked her if she would like a Rosary, and when she hesitated, he asked if she was Catholic. Her eyes filled with tears as she admitted that, yes, she was. Mike sat down with her, and for some time she just talked, sharing that she was suffering from severe headaches and was having trouble at work. She did not open up about her experience with Catholicism, yet it was clear that having someone really listen to her concerns had softened her heart. Near the end of their conversation, Mike spoke to her about God's mercy—that no wrong is so great that God will not forgive the sinner and give him peace. Before she left, Mike had not only given her a Rosary, but also pamphlets, CDs, a Miraculous Medal, and information on the Divine Mercy. She told Mike, "I know God put you here for me today!" He then gave her some holy water for blessing herself, which had come from the shrine of Our Lady of Lourdes in France where so many miracles have occurred. As she walked away, Mike and I prayed the Divine Mercy Chaplet for her.

A few weeks later the woman stopped by again. She had quit her job and would be leaving Las Vegas to start over. She thanked us for being out on the Strip that day, and for being willing to listen without judgment.

Sometimes it is not a lost soul who crosses our path, but someone who simply needs encouragement. This was the case the day we spoke to a family from Hawaii who shared that they were Catholics and on vacation in Las Vegas, leaving a tragic situation at home. Three days before they left, their house had burned down. "We need to start over when we go back, but since the trip had already been paid for, we decided to take our vacation anyway," the father told us.

"I am so sorry to hear about your home and am glad to see that you are all unhurt. Would you like some Rosaries?" Mike said.

"Sure! This will be the start of our family praying a Rosary together each day. Thank you," the father replied as Mike handed them each a colorful set of beads. We know that the power of family prayer, and the Rosary in particular, is so great that miracles can happen and holiness grows where it is practiced. Situations like these have helped me to see the need to meet people where they are, never assuming or judging, just offering hope and a willingness to listen. It is amazing what fruits come from this type of approach!

Being in Las Vegas, we have quite a few Mormons pass by our table. I have had an interest in Mormonism since college when I read a book about a man who left the Mormon faith when he learned the Mormon teaching on abortion. He understood the truth of the Catholic teaching that all life is sacred and valued from the first moment. I was in awe of the faith of a man who was able to see the truth and believe it. How unlike me, who had lived with the true faith for twenty years before God opened my eyes!

One Saturday, a man covered in tattoos came to our table. He told me he was a Mormon who had some questions about the "errors" of Catholic teaching.

"You know your Church fell into a great apostasy when the apostle John died," he stated bluntly.

I was a little taken aback by such a clearly false statement, but I knew better than to jump right into a heated debate. Instead, I asked him to explain more of his understanding of the matter. When he finished, I posed a question.

"Does it make sense," I asked, "that Jesus would establish His Church and then leave it in error for sixteen hundred years?" We looked at Matthew 16:18–19 where Jesus founds the Church on Peter the rock and gives him the authority to bind and to loose. Slowly I brought the conversation around to the early Church councils that confirmed the books of the Bible. When he began to see that the canon of the Bible itself rested on the authority of the bishops, he seemed a little less sure of his claims. At the end of the conversation he left saying, "Wow! You got my head spinning!" We again prayed for our new acquaintance as he left—that he would continue seeking the truth.

In people like this young man, it is easy to see myself shortly after my reconversion—reading, studying, eagerly trying to find out the truth, and in the process, growing closer to our Lord. Street evangelization shows me the many paths that people take to find God, and the great humility of our God who meets each person on his individual path to bring him to His heart. He does not shrink from the messiest life, the most sinful habits, even those of an arrogant twenty-year-old who thought he was strong enough on his own. Truly, Jesus' Divine Mercy is overwhelming!

BEAUTY

"If anyone asks you about your faith, take him to church and show him the icons", Saint John Chrysostom is reported to have said. How many times does the beauty of a thing capture us and draw us toward itself? Early in my conversion, I found myself attracted to the beauty of the Church, in its art and liturgy and in the lives of those who live their faith well. Now I've come to realize that the great beauty of God and His Bride, the Church, is a powerful tool for evangelization.

Once, I spoke with a young couple vacationing in Las Vegas who I learned had three unbaptized children, although the father had been raised Catholic. My apologetics training prompted me to jump right in with the facts about how baptism removes original sin, yet I could see that another approach might have more of an impact. So I began to tell them about some of the amazing contributions Catholics have made in the areas of art and science: how thirty-two of the craters on the moon are named after Jesuit priests; how the Catholic Church feeds, educates, and shelters more people every day than any other institution on earth; and how the Church actually began the first hospitals and universities. By the end of our conversation, the wife looked quizzically at her husband and said, "So why aren't our kids baptized?" They asked for some of our pamphlets containing further information on Catholicism, and we happily complied. Some people need to hear about a moral teaching of the Church, and some have a question about doctrine that has been troubling them, but many more folks just need to know that the Church we belong to is good and beautiful and has a powerful transformative presence in the world.

THE WORK OF THE HOLY SPIRIT

Being a street evangelist has been both humbling and rewarding. Every day, we reach hundreds of people. Many walk right by us, yet even they might be touched simply by our presence. Each encounter is unique, as each soul has a particular relationship with the Lord. One day, as I was taking stock of our supplies, I was shocked to discover that we had given away nearly eight thousand Rosaries on the streets of Las Vegas in a little less than a year! We pray and hope that those who receive them are open to the grace of the Holy Spirit in their lives, and we are grateful to play even a little part in God's work.

Working with Mike has helped reveal to me how hungry people are for God's love. And it is only when they accept this that they are able to listen openly to the Church's teaching on various controversial topics. Sometimes, I share my story—how when I lived a life of sin, I was completely immersed in selfishness, but then God worked powerfully in my life and turned my worldview upside down. I tell them that in those early days following my great act of contrition, I clung to the Ten Commandments and the Beatitudes because they were the guidelines I needed to know in order to live rightly—to think of others rather than myself. I knew instinctively that those rules were for my good and showed God's love for me. When I share this with people, they know that I am sincere and can often be led to see God's love for them in a similar way.

Before people leave our table, we make sure we hand them something tangible. This is a great sales technique, but it also means that they will have something physical—a Rosary, a medal, a holy card—that they can touch and see and that can draw them to God. Whenever they see it on their desk or kitchen counter, they will remember that God is waiting. We are the sowers of the seed, but the Holy Spirit does the work of nurturing the seed for a rich harvest. Can there be any greater joy than knowing we have served the Lord in bringing another wayward soul back to Christ?

Chapter 7

The Flint Mission Project

Adam Janke

Flint, Michigan

A woman with a cane and hunched shoulders ambled toward the corner of West First Street and Saginaw in downtown Flint, Michigan, where a St. Paul Street Evangelization team had set up its materials for a day of proclaiming the good news.

"Would you like a free Rosary?" Paul called to the woman as he walked toward her, a slew of Rosaries draped over his arm.

She stopped at the sound of his voice and turned slightly. "What was that?"

"Would you like a Rosary? They're free."

The woman looked up at him. "Why, sure. Thank you, young man."

"Do you know how to pray the Rosary?" Paul asked as he handed her a yellow one. She shook her head, and Paul opened a small pamphlet he had extracted from his pocket and held it before her. "This diagram shows which prayers to say as you hold each bead of the Rosary. And here on the back are all the prayers. So on this bead, you say an 'Our Father' and on each of these ten, you say a 'Hail Mary'. And while you're saying those prayers, you think about different events in the life of Jesus and His Mother."

"Well now, thank you, young man. I know I would have to study that to get it right."

"No problem," Paul said. "It can take practice, I know. Go ahead and keep that pamphlet." He refolded it and handed it to her. "Is there anything you would like us to pray for? My friends and I here are praying for whatever people ask us to."

Suddenly, the woman pressed her hand to her mouth. She looked away then pulled a tissue from her handbag and began to dab at her eyes. At that moment, another SPSE team member walked up.

"Hi, I'm Kelly—oh, what's wrong?"

"This morning I was at court," the woman stammered, "just leaving the courthouse now. See, my landlady, she wants to evict me. She doesn't like me and just wants me out. I don't know what I'm going to do or where I'm going to go. And, I'm sick! I can't be out on the streets when I'm sick!" She stopped, unable to continue, her hand pressed again to her mouth.

"Oh, I'm so sorry to hear that!" Kelly exclaimed.

Paul said, "Can we pray with you right now?"

The woman sniffed, nodded, and bowed her head. Paul opened his St. Paul Street Evangelization pocket handbook and led a prayer, asking Jesus to act in the life of this woman. He entrusted her to our Lord's care and protection and also asked that her landlady's heart be softened.

At the end of the prayer, the woman was visibly calmer. Paul and Kelly continued to encourage her and remind her of Jesus' love and constant concern for what happens to her. After several minutes of conversation, the woman blew her nose, looked up, and smiled at Paul and Kelly. "You know, you young people are really what I needed this morning," she said. "That prayer is what I needed to hear. I know my sweet Jesus will take care of me."

"He sure will! And we will definitely pray for you," Kelly assured her.

"Thank you both so much." The woman smiled again. "I have to go now and catch my bus."

This one small encounter, this one small miracle of three people coming together who did not know each other, establishing a relationship, and sharing God's saving work in their lives is the essence of evangelization.

There was something unique about the street evangelization team that went out that day. It was composed of teenagers.

In the summer of 2013 I was approached by a group of youth ministers in the Diocese of Lansing, Michigan, who were preparing to put on an annual service camp for teens called the "Flint Mission Project". During the service camp, the teens would do basic repairs, paint, pull weeds, and clean for the residents of the economically depressed city of Flint, collaborating with groups like Habitat for Humanity and Catholic Charities. The Mission also had a retreat component with times for Mass, confession, and Eucharistic Adoration.

I worked with most of the Mission's organizers in my role as Director of Religious Education at Saint Mary. They knew that I was heavily involved with St. Paul Street Evangelization and asked if I would consider taking a group of teens and training them in street evangelization.

Whoa! SPSE had never trained high school students before, and I wasn't sure how they would respond both to the training and to the actual street evangelization. At first I was hesitant, but on further consideration, I figured we had nothing to lose. Young David slew Goliath, right? Why not let the teens have a try? The other youth ministers and I decided that we would let all the teens who were interested in evangelizing put their names in a hat, and we would draw a few of those names to train with me during the first day of the camp.

TRAINING

The first step for our teen evangelists was to take our newly formed Teen Encounter Workshop. It worked much like our adult Basic Evangelization Training in that it was not just for those who are going to evangelize on the street, but instead we focused on the basic principles of what it means to be a missionary disciple in any circumstance. Pope Francis lays out these principles in his Apostolic Exhortation, *Evangelii gaudium*, emphasizing that all people are called to evangelize by virtue of their baptism, and that feeling inadequate is not an excuse to "postpone the evangelizing mission".[1] The Teen Encounter was modified especially for young people, and we spent a lot of time studying the stories of young Catholic role models, such as Blessed Pier Giorgio Frassati.

During the training day we encouraged the teens to break the ice and get to know one another, and we tried to pull them slowly out of their comfort zones just as we did for our adult evangelists. Catholics

[1] Francis, *Evangelii gaudium*, The Joy of the Gospel, November 24, 2013 (Vatican City: Libreria Editrice Vaticana), no. 121.

are generally very reticent about sharing their faith with other people because we live in a secular culture of religious silence, marked by the mistaken notion that faith is a private, personal matter. Even very holy, faith-filled people can struggle to share the gospel out of a fear that they might offend someone. The pervasive cultural view is one of relativism, that one religion is as good as another, so why should anyone question *my* religious views and—heaven forbid—suggest that I change? The teens had the same questions our adult trainees did: Will people reject me? Is our presence really welcome on the street? Will I be yelled at? What if I don't have all the answers to the questions people ask? In the training, we addressed these concerns and explained that the real-life experience of street evangelization is very different from what nearly everyone expects it to be. Much of that has to do with our nonconfrontational approach. Instead of being annoyed with us, people thank us for our presence time and time again.

Our first exercise in training was to have the teens share any story they wanted to, in two to three minutes, enthusiastically. They could tell us the plot to the movie *Toy Story*, how to make a pizza, or how to take a nap in math class, as long as it was done really, *really* enthusiastically. By going overboard in the training, they were more likely to speak up and smile when they are on the street. When I was taught how to be a lector at Mass, our deacon had us practice reading twice as slowly as we should when actually proclaiming the Word. That way, when we were nervous at the ambo at Mass, we would read at an appropriate pace instead of too fast because the pace we had practiced was excessively slow.

The teens had a great time "going overboard", and it really helped those who were more inclined to be introverts. I hear from a lot of introverts that they can't do street evangelization, but I am an introvert myself. I need to get to know people and feed off the energy of my friends before I am talkative. I still become nervous once in a while when I do street evangelization, and that's okay. Yet, with practice and the right set of tools, introverts make extraordinary evangelists and tend to be better at listening and empathy than our more extroverted counterparts. Introverts, get out there and evangelize!

Enthusiasm is just one of a dozen areas that the teens practiced. We taught them how to identify where people were in their journeys to God, how to share the story of salvation, how to share their own personal testimonies, and how to pray with others. As they practiced all these areas, their confidence-meters rose. The practice proved invaluable when they got out on the street, and then they kept practicing by doing.

Finally, we equipped all our evangelists with information on how to point people in the right direction to get material help from the Church through organizations like the St. Vincent de Paul Society.

STORIES FROM THE STREET

I love stories from the very first time a new evangelization team goes out. The Holy Spirit always seems to encourage them by allowing them to see the fruits of their labor, as when Paul and Kelly received affirmation that their presence and words comforted a woman who was distressed and scared. Kelly commented to me later that, while they might not see people's lives changed in dramatic ways every time they evangelize, getting a little bit of affirmation was fantastic and fulfilling.

It shouldn't come as a surprise that the Holy Spirit wants to encourage His disciples when they share the faith. After all, that is our role as disciples. And, of course, it is not our work, but that of the Holy Spirit, who is the principal agent of evangelization. It is a great relief to have this knowledge! Without God, I can do nothing and have nothing to offer, but with the help of the Holy Spirit, conversions and miracles abound. Why do we think so little of the promises of the New Testament? When we read the book of Acts and see the courage with which the apostles and all those called by God went forth after Pentecost (cf. Acts 4:13, 33), we should be confident in our own evangelization, grounded in the strength and efficacy of the Spirit of God.

One of the teens, Dan, received a particularly powerful gift of encouragement from the Holy Spirit. Dan is an introvert, and although he was excited about evangelizing, when he showed up on the street the first day, a wave of anxiety hit him. He only managed to speak briefly with a few people. He left the street at the end of the day, disappointed in himself and feeling that he had let God down. I heartily commend Dan for what he did next. He could have sulked or gathered a pity party around him or just given up. Instead, he spent the better part of the evening in Adoration, asking for the gift of the Holy Spirit so that during the rest of the week he would be able to evangelize without fear. The next day out on the street, Dan's anxiety returned. However, he persevered, and after forty-five minutes, he found himself initiating conversations the way he never expected that he would. He even led some people through the "Prayer of Consecration to Jesus Christ". Later Dan told me that he felt like a vessel of the Holy Spirit and knew that "it was completely God acting through me because I would never act like that in any other circumstance."

The evangelist can be just as much a recipient of God's grace as the evangelized, if he is open to the gift, as Dan was during his own "Pentecost moment".

Dan's story also highlights the very human element of street evangelization. Even with the training, a lot of the teens were still apprehensive at first. Bayley told me that she was excited to get out on the street, but she was really nervous, too. She wanted to talk to the first person right away because she knew it would be easier once she started talking to people. She was right. After her first few conversations, the nervousness went away, and she started having fun. Every single one of the teens said it was more than worth it to get over the nervousness for the reward of the experience of evangelizing.

On the very first day of evangelization during the 2013 Flint Mission Project, the Holy Spirit gave us a huge boost of encouragement. We set up our materials, invoked the Lord's blessing on the day, and the teens were off. Two of the adult volunteers with us that day, Nancy and Theresa, who had never evangelized on the street before, were also willing to jump right in.

"Oh, look! Here's our first person," Theresa said to Nancy, and we all turned to where Theresa was looking. A man was walking toward us who, frankly, I considered to be the least likely of anyone to accept the gospel. He was covered in tattoos, had a bald head, and wore large gauge earrings. What I was actually thinking was, "If anyone is going to punch us in the face, it's this guy."

Theresa and Nancy stepped out from behind the table to approach the stranger. I wasn't exactly worried, but I made a mental promise to keep an eye on that conversation no matter what else I became involved in. But what happened next blew us all away.

"Good morning, sir," called Theresa. "Would you like a free Rosary?"

The man seemed caught off guard, looked intently at the Rosary, then said as though a light were dawning on him, "Hey, are you guys *Catholic*?"

"Yep, we sure are," said Theresa. "And what about you, sir? Do you profess any certain religion?"

"I have been a Buddhist my whole life, but I just finished reading the *Catechism of the Catholic Church*."

Say what? We were stunned. I don't think I know any *Catholics* who have read the whole *Catechism*.

We talked to the man for over an hour. He had many questions about Catholicism and was particularly interested in the Incarnation of Jesus and the Catholic approach to suffering. I just couldn't get over this encounter. What are the chances of meeting someone who is interested in the Catholic faith, has questions, and has just finished reading the entire *Catechism of the Catholic Church*? And you just happened to have allotted four hours of that particular day to talking about the Catholic Church?

The encounter certainly was a gift of encouragement from the Holy Spirit and a lesson to us all—especially me—in not being judgmental.

Our Buddhist friend was very open to the truth of our explanations and seemed to have a deep appreciation for the logic, cohesion, and beauty of Catholicism. Finally, someone asked him point blank—what was keeping him from becoming Catholic? He replied that nothing was, now that we had answered his questions. Unbelievable! Who but the Holy Spirit could have orchestrated such a meeting of the right people at the right time? He asked us to put him in touch with a Catholic church so he could take the next step. We contacted the local RCIA director and got the two of them together.

Unfortunately, as time went on I lost touch with the man, but a year later while evangelizing with the teens during the 2014 Flint Mission, we ran into him again. He told us that he was still open to God and the Catholic faith, but he had not yet received the sacraments or officially entered the Church.

Some people might call that a failure, but we know that success is not measured by the people we meet who end up becoming Catholic. A better measure of success is our openness to what God is asking us to do and our faithfulness to Him in doing it. According to Blessed Teresa of Calcutta, "God doesn't ask that we succeed in everything, but that we are faithful. However beautiful our work may be, let us not become attached to it. Always remain prepared to give it up, without losing your peace."[2] Yes, we would love to have heard that this young man

[2]Jaya Chaliha and Edward Le Joly, *The Joy in Loving: A Guide to Daily Living* (New Delhi: Penguin Books, 1996), p. 334.

had gone through RCIA and was received into the Church last Easter, but the fact that he wasn't shouldn't discourage us. A healthy degree of detachment fosters humility and helps us to remember that this is ultimately God's work, not ours.

There have been times that I have done street evangelization when the entire day seems *dry*. There are no particularly good conversations, and sometimes we run into people who do want to argue or do not take well to our presence. It doesn't happen often, but it does happen. This again is an opportunity to be faithful without having any evident signs of success, an opportunity to hang onto your peace and just keep doing what God is asking you to do.

The teens, however, seemed to have virtually no dry days. I think there is something about sincere, young people evangelizing that really touches people somehow. So many passersby walked up to our teens with their hurts, with their questions, and with their hunger for the truth. The teens were thanked over and over again for their ministry.

Taylor and Bryce were in a conversation with a woman who happened to mention that she was a Protestant pastor. Taylor gulped. What did she, a sixteen-year-old Catholic, have to offer to a woman who has made it her life's work to lead and teach other Protestants? At first she was a little overwhelmed and afraid that she wouldn't know enough. She persevered, however, and soon found herself having a wonderful conversation about the Eucharist. The pastor accepted some CDs containing Catholic talks and said she was very impressed by the non-confrontational street evangelization these young Catholics were doing. When Bryce asked if the pastor had any prayer intentions, they ended up praying together on the street, and Taylor was touched that the pastor prayed for them and the other street evangelists as well. The encounter showed Taylor the openness of the community to the presence of the evangelists and that the community had something to offer them, too. She realized that we are able to recognize each other's dignity and hope for each other's good even when we have disagreements.

CALLING DOWN DIVINE MERCY ON FLINT

The teens were dogged in seeking prayer requests. They fastidiously recorded them in notebooks, taking down names and details. By the end of the week of the 2013 Flint Mission, they had collected three hundred prayer requests. *For Ethel's daughter who is a heroin addict, that Latisha can get food stamps so she can feed her babies, for Middy who is diabetic and has gangrene in his foot, that Crystal's son will get out of prison soon and find the Lord.*

Flint, Michigan, was named the country's most dangerous city for three years in a row, 2010–2012.[3] The outsourcing of the auto industry that began in the early '80s robbed the formerly thriving hub of its backbone. Many residents moved out as unemployment, poverty, and crime crept in.

The community they encountered during the week of the Flint Mission was one most of our teens were not used to. They were struck by the brokenness, desperation, and injustice in the stories people told them, but also impressed by the hopeful tenacity and roll-with-the-punches attitudes still flickering and sparking in the midst of difficult lives.

It was the end of the afternoon on the last day of the 2013 Flint Mission. A couple of adult leaders, eight teens, and I were making our way back to our vehicles from the University of Michigan-Flint campus where we had been evangelizing. The teens would be headed to Saint Mary, Queen of Angels, a parish ten miles away where they had been staying during the Mission. They would shower, eat, and enjoy an evening of recapping the week, fellowship, and prayer.

Whew! It had been an awesome but draining week, and I myself was looking forward to a mindless, quiet, hour-long ride home with the AC blasting and a can of diet soda. When I got there, I would eat dinner, play with the kids a little, do an hour or so of work, and maybe go to bed early. Then tomorrow—

"Hey, Adam, can we do something?" Taylor called from behind me where she and the other teens had been walking and talking in an excited clump.

"What? What do you mean?" I asked.

"I mean, can we do something about these?" She held up a blue spiral notebook that I knew contained prayer intentions collected during the week.

[3] Annmargaret Warner, Erin Fuchs, and Gus Lubin, "The 25 Most Dangerous Cities in America", *Business Insider*, June 13, 2013, http://www.businessinsider.com/most-dangerous-cities-in-america-2013-6.

"We want to do something about them right now," Brian said. "We want to pray right now."

I was already starting my weekend in my mind, but these teens weren't finished. Their prayer-request notebooks were burning holes in their pockets.

I looked at the other two adult leaders who shrugged. "Well, sure," I said, knowing that this was not on the evening's schedule, "why don't we find a church?"

Saint Michael's was the closest Catholic church to the university campus, and it had a Eucharistic Chapel. Once inside, I soon found out that it wasn't enough for each of us to pray individually. The teens wanted more.

"Let's pray the Divine Mercy Chaplet together," Bryce urged.

"Let's sing it!"

Wow, these teens were going all in. Reluctant to lead the difficult chant a capella, I was relieved when someone else volunteered to do it.

There before our Lord in the Blessed Sacrament, we lifted up to Him His children we had encountered that week in all their various circumstances. From my spot near the back of the chapel, I watched the teens flip through their notebooks, bringing their eyes from the pages to the tabernacle, invoking the mercy of Jesus to shower upon "us and on the whole world." I marveled at the fervor, sincerity, single-mindedness, and maturity of these teens who chose to postpone their pizza dinner and reunion with their friends in order to initiate a time of earnest intercession for the people who had touched their lives during the Mission.

This spontaneous prayer time set a precedent. The following year, the teens considered it a given that on the last day of the Mission they should intercede for the people they had met that week. This time, all ninety kids of the entire Mission took part, not just the eight or ten who had done street evangelization. The teens took the hundreds of prayer requests and prayed for each person by name, followed by the recitation of the Rosary in the presence of our Lord in Eucharistic Adoration.

"LET NO ONE DESPISE YOUR YOUTH"

Now that we have been training and sending teens out to evangelize at the Flint Mission for two years in a row, I cannot tell you how immensely proud I am of them. I am certain they have changed countless lives in

Flint, and many teens have attested to how the experience of evangelization has impacted their own lives. Street evangelization has helped them to grow—both in their faith and personally. It brings them out of themselves. Kelly said, "Sometimes you forget that you're not the only one out there with problems. You're not the only one who needs prayer." They have told me that street evangelization challenges them—iron sharpens iron—to know their faith better because others are asking questions about it, and it has strengthened their prayer lives, too.

Some teens have even continued to evangelize with our SPSE teams outside of the service camp. But virtually all of them have used their experiences on the street to evangelize in the circumstances of their everyday lives. They are now better equipped to share their faith with their family and friends and anyone else the Holy Spirit sends their way.

It seems as though Pope Francis might have had young people in mind when he wrote, "All the baptized, whatever their position in the Church or their level of instruction in the faith, are agents of evangelization, and it would be insufficient to envisage a plan of evangelization to be carried out by professionals while the rest of the faithful would simply be passive recipients."[4]

Our teens certainly are not professionals, but they are baptized, and that is more important! They have elected not to "be passive recipients", but are active members of the Body of Christ, willing to share their excitement and zeal for the gospel with others, many of whose "hearts ... are gripped by fear and desperation, even in the so-called rich countries."[5]

Saint Paul knew the essential role of young people in the Church when he exhorted Timothy, "Let no one despise your youth, but set the believers an example in speech and conduct, in love, in faith, in purity" (1 Tim 4:12). Now St. Paul Street Evangelization knows it, too.

[4] Francis, *Evangelii gaudium*, no. 120.

[5] Ibid., no. 52.

Chapter 8

A Catholic Notch in the Bible Belt

Paul Mathers

Dallas, Texas

"You're all going to hell! You need to be saved! Read the Bible! Read John 3:16!"

The man was using a bullhorn and shouting at Catholics as they exited their parish church after Sunday Mass. I had come across the YouTube video while searching for information about Catholic outreach.

My training and years as a police officer helped me keep my emotions in check. And I was fascinated. Although the man was misguided and misinformed, I admired his zeal. He was so eager and so determined to save those poor "pagan" Catholics. He had taken his own free time and gone down to the church on a Sunday in an effort to save the people. His approach, though, seemed ineffective. I watched the video again.

This time, I paid attention to the reactions of the Catholics as they came out of Mass. As desperately as the street preacher wanted to convert them, he didn't realize that he was getting only negative attention. Most of the people just ignored him—absolutely the worst thing that can happen to a speaker. Some, though, did give him dirty looks—which at least indicated that they heard him.

However, no presence of the love of Jesus Christ was evident either in the man's message or in his manner, nothing that would attract anyone. Instead, his approach had too much anger, too much aggression, and too much negativity. There also seemed to be no room for talking with him, except perhaps to say, "Okay, what do I do now?" Therefore, as good as the man's intentions had been, I concluded that he had succeeded only in making people uncomfortable.

However, the video started me wondering. Did the Catholic Church have a less aggressive way to evangelize in public? I searched the Internet, and the search engine quickly brought up the St. Paul Street Evangelization site. There on the homepage, I read its mission statement:

> St. Paul Street Evangelization is a grassroots, non-profit Catholic evangelization organization, dedicated to responding to the mandate of Jesus to preach the Gospel to all nations by taking our Catholic Faith to the streets. We do this in a non-confrontational way, allowing the Holy Spirit to move in the hearts of those who witness our public Catholic presence.

My eyes locked onto the word "non-confrontational". After examining everything on the apostolate's site, I knew: this is what I wanted to do. SPSE evangelists reach out in love with no judgments, no prejudices, and no aggression.

OPENED EYES

My search for Catholic outreach was one link in a chain of efforts to live my Catholic faith fully. The first major link had occurred about fifteen years earlier when our teenaged daughter, Pamela, started dating a Baptist. My wife and I hadn't seen a crisis coming. Yes, Karen and I knew that many people called Dallas the "buckle" of the Bible Belt. Yes, we knew that meant that most people here were Baptists. Neither were we surprised when Pamela told us a Baptist boy would be taking her out. What we never expected, however, was that the young man would seriously challenge our daughter's Catholic faith.

Right away, Pamela approached us with a list of questions. "Why do we go to confession to a priest? Do we really believe we are eating Jesus Christ when we go to Communion? Why do we pray to saints? Why do we worship Mary?"

Karen and I looked at each other. We had no idea how to answer those questions. We just did and believed things because that was what Catholics did and believed.

I had not, though, been raised Catholic. I was baptized Lutheran as a baby, but my family left that community when I was still very young. My mother later tried to get me involved in the Unity Church. I refused, however, to pay any attention at its services. Therefore, I grew up essentially unchurched. That all changed in my early twenties, when I met my wife-to-be, Karen. There was a wholesomeness in that petite, strong young woman that made me realize that my life was missing something important, something God-centered. We began to date and, soon, to plan marriage. Since she and her family were all Catholic, I decided to become Catholic as well. From then on, we attended Mass every Sunday and felt satisfied that we understood and were living out our Catholic faith.

Now, however, it had suddenly become urgent that we find answers to our daughter's questions—and not just for Pamela's sake. Although her relationship with her Baptist boyfriend was brief, its impact on our family lasted.

Karen and Pamela decided to take a class at Saint Michael's Catholic Church in Garland, Texas. It was on apologetics—that area of study concerned with defending the faith. The shift I was then working kept me from attending the class with them, but my wife and daughter came home and shared with me everything they learned. Soon we knew how to answer the Baptist objections.

We learned that we confess our sins to a priest and believe that Jesus is truly present in Holy Communion because that's what He taught us to do and believe. We ask the saints to pray for us because Christians should pray for each other, and even death does not separate us from Christ. And, while we always offer worship to God alone, we honor Mary because Jesus does.

Of course, those answers barely touched on the wealth of solid reasoning that stood behind each teaching. There was more, so much more! Our whole family felt as if entire floodgates of delight had suddenly opened wide before us. The more we understood the Catholic faith, the more we felt overwhelmed and inspired by the richness it contained, both in sacred Scripture and in tradition. We discovered people such as Scott Hahn, Patrick Madrid, and Dave Armstrong. Then we learned about the broadcasts from the Eternal Word Television Network (EWTN) and Catholic Answers, and we drew inspiration from those, too.

For the next few years, I studied as I never had before. Then, with the development of the Internet, I found new and exciting ways to do research and learn the faith. I found so much peace and joy that I knew it must have been a gift from God. Karen and I (and, later, our daughter and her husband) became more and more involved with ministries at our parish and in apologetics.

As my faith deepened, so did my desire to do even more for the Catholic Church, to help others appreciate her truth and beauty. It was in September 2012 that I came across the YouTube video of the "bull-horn preacher" and then managed to find SPSE. In one of the most life-changing actions I ever took, I sent an e-mail and connected with Steve Dawson. He advised me to contact a Catholic friend of his, Arthur Kaye, who was living in Texas at the time. Arthur and I met for a cup of coffee and mapped out a plan for starting Catholic street evangelization in Dallas. Since our Lord advises us to "first sit down and count the cost" (Lk 14:28) before starting to build, this felt wise.

MISSION CONTROL

Arthur and I adopted SPSE's mission statement for the Dallas team. It stated *what* we would be trying to accomplish. Our assigned task was merely to plant the seeds. The subsequent growth and harvest would be up to the Holy Spirit.

What we could do, though, was make sure that our seeds received water. For this, we needed people dedicated to praying for the success of our efforts. It turns out that, in deciding to set up our prayer-support team first, I was following some giant footprints. At the turn of the thirteenth century, Saint Dominic accepted the mission of ending the Albigensian heresy in southern France and bringing the heretics back home to the Catholic faith. To do this, it is said, the first thing he did was establish a monastery for cloistered nuns. These holy women agreed to shut themselves away from the pleasures of the world to dedicate their lives entirely to praying for the success of Saint Dominic's preaching friars. The religious order he founded still exists, known today as the Dominicans. Arthur and I made a note that setting up the prayer-support team had to be our first priority.

Our next step was to look at the qualifications for people who might want to join our team of Catholic street evangelists after we got it launched. Our bottom line was that they would have to be good, solid, practicing Catholics with a love for Jesus Christ and His Church. They certainly didn't need to be professional apologists.

That decided, we briefly sketched out our list of needed supplies. SPSE currently makes available an abundance of support materials for the Catholic street evangelist: signs, pamphlets, books, CDs, prayer cards, Rosaries, and more. At that time, though, all they had to offer were the sandwich-board signs. We decided to order one and to obtain the Rosaries, pamphlets, and other supplies elsewhere.

Now all we needed to decide was where to hold our first evangelization outing. A location with heavy foot traffic was essential. We picked Rockwall, an upscale northeastern suburb of Dallas, located on the eastern shore of Lake Ray Hubbard. Additionally, Rockwall would soon be hosting an outdoor barbecue cook-off. It was ideal.

I ordered the sign, some Rosaries, Miraculous Medals, CDs, and pamphlets. We also made sure we had our prayer-support team in place. Our first team member was a Byzantine Catholic woman, who committed to pray for us, for our work, and for all those who met us. Then the Legion of Mary in Dallas also committed themselves to supporting us with their prayers. (Since then, many, many more committed prayer warriors have joined in backing the efforts of our SPSE evangelists.)

FIRST OUTINGS

Soon enough, the day of the Rockwall barbecue arrived. Arthur and I found a shady spot on the town square near the cook-off. We eagerly set up our table and placed the Rosaries on one side and a stand holding pamphlets about Catholic teachings on the other. To the side of the table, we set up our sign.

We felt a little nervous. However, we also trusted that God would be with us. At first, people looked at us Catholics as though we were aliens. Most of them were either Baptists or other Bible-only Christians. But then people began to stop and talk with us. By the end of the day, we no longer worried about any funny looks we might receive. That first day was pretty uneventful, and it showed us that, hey, we could actually do this! It also whet our appetite for more street evangelization.

Since that first occasion, I have continued to go out regularly to evangelize. On one day, when evangelist Gene Tobola was with me, our final encounter impressed upon us the powerful influence of the Rosary. Just as we were considering packing up to return home, an enthusiastic woman ran up to us exclaiming, "Oh, I love the Rosary!"

"These are free. Help yourself," Gene said.

"Thank you so much!"

"Which parish do you attend?" I asked.

After grabbing a Rosary, she hurried on her way, tossing a parting remark over her shoulder. "I'm not Catholic. I am a nondenominationalist."

Gene and I glanced at each other, puzzled. Who knows how Mary would touch that woman's heart, and the hearts of the others we met? Who knows how, through the graces of the Rosary, each will be drawn closer to the heart of her Son, Jesus Christ? God works in mysterious ways. We have seen repeatedly, though, that non-Catholics as well as Catholics like the Rosary.

BLASTOFF

In a very short time, we had eight chapters in the Dallas area. It was like, "BOOM! BOOM! BOOM!" Someone from our area would contact SPSE, Steve would have the potential evangelist contact me, and then—SNAP!—we had another team set up. In what seemed like no time at all, we had a second Dallas team, then ones in Anna, Allen/McKinney, Copperas Cove, Tyler, Fort Worth, and North Dallas.

We simply explained what we did and offered people an opportunity to come out with us to experience Catholic street evangelization for themselves. Afterward—if they planned to continue with us—we helped them with training and setting up on their own. Each of our teams decides on its own venues and times to evangelize. My own team goes out about once a month.

SPSE's Steve Dawson tells me that the Dallas network is unique within the SPSE organization, that there is no other region in the country with so many teams in a single metropolis that actively collaborate with each other. Within the "Dallas SPSE conglomerate", a sense of camaraderie exists, forming the basis for our teamwork, fellowship, and connectedness. We foster this by occasionally gathering the whole Dallas-area organization together for a potluck or barbecue cookout. Besides helping mutual friendships to develop, the occasions become a great way to inspire each other and exchange ideas. Of course, we also enjoy telling and hearing about each other's evangelization experiences. We all seek and share Christ's great love and mercy. This binds us together and keeps us encouraged.

Besides building and supporting our teams, the Dallas SPSE organization also takes steps to let all the Catholics in the area know about our street evangelization efforts. A local Catholic radio host, Dave Palmer, has interviewed us several times. The station also plays SPSE Public Service Announcements. I am also in contact with the Dallas diocesan newspaper, *The Texas Catholic.* In fact, reporters from all the various media sometimes contact us. We always invite them to go evangelizing with us, and their resulting stories reach a wide audience. Our most current project is the plan to go to each of the Catholic parishes in the area and personally present SPSE to its pastor. Our hope, then, is that he will allow us to talk to his congregation about Catholic street evangelization, set up our table after Mass, put an article in the bulletin, or otherwise engage his parishioners.

OSCAR CAVAZOS

Our Lord has blessed the Dallas SPSE organization with a wide variety of evangelists. We have different strengths, come from widely differing backgrounds, and belong to different age groups. Each of us, however, has the same passion for Jesus Christ and His Church. This section introduces one of the people who joined me early in our street evangelization work in Dallas, Oscar Cavazos. While I considered myself solidly Catholic ever since I decided to join the Church, Oscar had a somewhat different journey. He is the owner of a local restaurant, a husband, and the father of three young children.

Although baptized Catholic as an infant, Oscar grew up in an area of Texas with no nearby Catholic church or mission. Thus, attending Mass was a rare event for his family. Neither was Catholic education available, and so no one could answer Oscar's questions about Catholic practices.

"Why do we sometimes stand and sometimes kneel at Mass?"

"Because we are Catholics."

"Why do we kiss the crucifix?"

"Because we are Catholics."

"Why do we pray the Rosary?"

"Because we are Catholics."

Deeply dissatisfied, young Oscar concluded to himself that, because no one could *give* him the reason for what they were doing, there *must be* no reason for it. Hence, a lifelong quest for solid reasons for faith took root in his soul.

At the time, though, his frustration only led him to dismiss Catholicism as mere superstition. In college, a similar frustration over all of the disagreements and contradictions among the various denominations of other Christians extended his rejection to Christianity as a whole. He then embraced what he called "happy agnosticism", deciding that it didn't matter whether he believed in Jesus or not.

Years later, though, he and his wife hit rock bottom. Their firstborn son hovered between life and death at the local hospital, and then Oscar lost his job. Driven to his knees in desperation, Oscar cried out for mercy from the God he didn't think he believed in. And God answered. Their son "outgrew" his medical condition, Oscar's business prospects fell into place, and soon they were in a position to help others.

Overwhelmed now by gratitude and love, Oscar hungered to get to know God. But the more he learned, the more his hunger grew. This time, though, the hunger itself was what helped him persevere as he began again the frustrating process of sifting through the contradictory teachings of the various denominations. His hunger drove him to keep searching for a truth that was solid enough to sustain him and his family.

Gifted with a love for research, he resolutely tackled each doctrinal issue until he had found a reasonable position—one that stood up under rigorous tests from both logic and from the Bible as a whole. On each issue, he came to recognize that only the Catholic teaching could withstand such honest scrutiny.

By this time, Oscar and his wife had joined a local Baptist congregation. They had found the community pleasant and welcoming, and they especially appreciated that there was a nursery available for their little ones. Oscar's wife was perfectly content, but Oscar soon began to have major disagreements with Baptist beliefs and practices. The desire began to stir to attend Mass once again.

Finally, he talked his wife into getting a babysitter and going with him to Midnight Mass on Christmas. When they arrived at the church, they didn't know what to expect but found that a helpful booklet had been placed in each pew. The Mass was beautiful. The entire church had been decorated with trees, flowers, and lights. Everything about it—the Mass, the music, and the carols—exuded the joy of the feast of Christmas. Joy to the World!

As he and his wife returned home that night, Oscar hungered for even more. Now he had begun to yearn to receive the Eucharist once again. He knew, though, that he would first have to be reconciled with the Catholic Church.

A couple of months later, he was ready. He made an appointment with the priest, and then, for the first time in seventeen years, Oscar entered a reconciliation room. He took with him a written list from his examination of conscience—two full pages.

To Oscar's surprise, the priest welcomed him warmly. He and Oscar talked for quite a long while, and never once did the priest scold or lecture or reprimand him. This, too, amazed Oscar. Then suddenly Oscar felt, right there in the confessional, a physical sensation as if Someone was tenderly wrapping a warm blanket around his shoulders! The experience convinced Oscar, now overwhelmed by emotion, that our Lord Himself was welcoming him home.

Soon afterward, Oscar attended a men's retreat at the parish. Then, a few months later, his non-Catholic wife surprised him by deciding to attend the women's retreat. Upon her return home, she urged Oscar to have their children baptized in the Catholic Church.

Once Oscar had returned to full communion with the Catholic Church, he began to experience a new call within his heart—the call to share the Catholic faith with others. He accepted a position as a catechist for seventh graders. But it was not enough. The call in his heart was deeper: he wanted to share the faith on a broad scale.

This is when he met me. It was shortly after I had founded the first Dallas SPSE chapter, so I invited Oscar to join us on our next outing. Like many prospective evangelists, he agreed to come "just to observe". Immediately, however, three young women stopped to talk with him—two were non-Catholic Christians and one was a fallen-away Catholic. Their conversation with Oscar continued for thirty minutes. During that time, he shared with them about some of the riches they could find in the Catholic Church, such as the Eucharist, confession, and Divine Mercy. By the end of that first conversation, Oscar had decided that

Catholic street evangelization was where he wanted to invest his time. He, too, had felt the same conviction that I had, "Hey, I can do this!" He has continued to work with the Dallas SPSE organization and is now head of our Allen/McKinney chapter.

STORIES FROM THE DALLAS AREA

On each SPSE outing, an evangelist might use several different approaches in order to reach people's hearts. Many of those who come to us are fallen-away Catholics, others are members of non-Catholic congregations but are curious about our materials, some are hurt and in need of comfort, and others are absolutely anti-Catholic. Not every encounter feels good, although many do. Neither is any encounter exactly like another. We hope, though, that the sampling that follows will give you a realistic sense of what it's really like to be a Catholic street evangelist. Many of the stories that follow were reported by Oscar.

One day in Allen, Texas, a woman approached the table that Oscar's SPSE team had set up. "Would you like a Rosary?" he asked her.

She stopped and looked at the Rosary, then reached out her hand and touched it. "I was baptized Catholic," she said, "but I had a very bad experience with the Church. I haven't been back since."

"I'm sorry," Oscar said. "Would you like to talk about it?"

She stood still a moment. But then she began her story. Oscar told us that, as she did, a heavy weight seemed to lift from her shoulders. "I haven't talked about this for years and years, but my sister passed away about twenty years ago," she said. "The Catholic Church was not very sympathetic. Our family didn't go to Mass very often, so we received no charity or empathy from the pastor. In fact, he rejected us." Then she repeated, "A priest rejected us in our distress!" The sadness, the bitterness, in her voice was unmistakable. "The only compassion we received," she said, "came from other denominations of Christians. They reached out to us in our grief."

Oscar softened his voice and tried to offer her some sympathetic advice. "If that happens, and you can't get help from a priest, you can go to the bishop and tell him your problems. Maybe he can help you understand and get you the help you need." Then he asked gently, "Have you ever thought about coming back to the Church?"

"No. I have been living too bad a life to come back to the Church," she said. "Anyway, my boyfriend would never let me."

"Jesus loves you so much," Oscar replied. "He is waiting for you. Whenever you are ready, you can come back." He gave her a Rosary and a pamphlet on how to say it. Then her boyfriend came to get her. She tensed immediately as he scolded, "What are you talking to these people for? Come on. We need to go! Hurry up and get back to the car." Then he walked away. The woman's eyes met Oscar's again briefly. She said good-bye, and he told her he would pray for her. To us he said that he prays that she will return to the Church someday and find the comforting mercy of Jesus. He hopes that she will find the joy and peace that seem to have eluded her all these years.

For a brief moment, Oscar had been able to help the woman begin to speak of her long-held grief. People are so hungry to connect person-to-person on a deep, spiritual level. As evangelists, we always hope to extend the love of Christ to each person we encounter. When we meet one of these lonely people, we take a real interest in who they are and what they are experiencing.

YOUNG DEFENDERS

On a brighter note, one day a woman came up to Oscar with her two little girls, who were about eight and four. When we offered them a Rosary, they eagerly began trying to choose among all of the different colors. Their mother told us that the older girl was preparing to receive her First Holy Communion. "She is not afraid to defend her faith in school," she added.

Oscar gave the older daughter a smile. "It's great that you love Jesus enough to defend His teachings," he said. "What happened at school that you had to defend the faith?"

"Well, one day at school, my friend asked me, 'Why do you care about Mary? Don't you realize she was nobody? It's all about Jesus!'" she told Oscar. Then she breathlessly continued, "So I asked her, 'Is your mother important to you? If your mom is important to you, how much more important do you think Jesus' mom is? We're supposed to respect our parents and I respect Mary, the Mother of Jesus.'"

Oscar congratulated her on her articulate defense of the faith. As she selected her Rosary from the table, she said, "My friend hasn't asked me any more questions about the things that Catholics do."

Oscar then encouraged her to continue defending the faith in that same loving and clear way. What a blessing to see parents working hard to teach their children both the doctrine and the practices of the Catholic Church.

FOR THE CHILDREN

On another day, a woman came by who had left the Church and joined a Baptist one. "Any church will do since we are all brothers and sisters in Christ," she stated. As she described the social groups, Bible study classes, and Sunday child care, Oscar began to wonder if she was attending the same Baptist church that his family had attended not so long ago. When he asked her about it, she said, "Yes, that's the one! How do you know about it?"

"Our family went to that church for a while," he said. "They're very welcoming and they have a lot of ways for people to interact with each other. However," he continued, "when they told me that I had to get baptized again as an adult—even though I had been baptized as an infant—I started doing some research." Then he said, "What I found was that the early Church Fathers approved and encouraged infant baptism!"

He then explained to the woman the Catholic teaching on infant baptism and quoted some passages of Scripture to support the teaching. "The more I studied the Church Fathers," Oscar told her, "the more I learned about the Catholic Church and the beauty of the sacraments and the devotional life."

"Yeah, I understand," she agreed. She turned to look at her children who were playing in the park.

"Have your children been baptized?" Oscar asked. She admitted that her older daughter had been baptized, but that her four-year-old had not. After explaining the importance of baptism, he asked her, "Do you want to have her baptized?"

For her to admit that, though, would mean that she would no longer accept the Baptist congregation's flawed understanding of Scripture. It would mean that she could no longer allow her children to be taught in their Sunday school. She would also no longer fit into their comfortable social circle, and so she would have to say good-bye to her Baptist church—and friends. She paused only a moment. Then she said, "Yes, I do want her baptized."

Of course, she would talk with her husband about it first, but her plan was to have her younger child baptized in the Catholic Church and to enroll her older daughter in CCD (Confraternity of Christian Doctrine) so that she could receive her First Holy Communion. Oscar recommended a Catholic church near her home and invited her to meet with the pastor about coming back to the Church. She left after that, asking us to pray for her and her children.

NOT SO EASY[1]

A unique event for Oscar occurred one day when Deacon Robert Holladay and he were evangelizing in a park. Earlier that morning, a Scripture verse had impressed itself upon Oscar's mind: "Always be prepared to make a defense to any one who calls you to account for the hope that is in you, yet do it with gentleness and reverence; and keep your conscience clear, so that, when you are abused, those who revile your good behavior in Christ may be put to shame" (1 Pet 3:15–16).

Oscar and Deacon Robert were setting up the SPSE table when they noticed another table, not too far away, where two men were talking to a young couple. Before long, the couple left and the two men made their way over to Oscar and the deacon, who greeted them and offered them each a Rosary.

"No!" they both said, with obvious distaste. The older man looked familiar, Oscar said later, but he couldn't figure out where he had seen him before.

Oscar asked, "Are you Catholic?"

"Not anymore," the man answered sharply. "I found Jesus and left the Catholic Church!"

Then Oscar recognized him. "I know who you are—you're Ralph S. Relitch! Oh, my gosh! I have watched all your videos on the Internet! This is amazing."

[1] For this story, we have changed names and other identifying features.

The man was a professional anti-Catholic preacher who worked aggressively to get Catholics to leave the Church. He took his message all over the country, even around the world. It was during Oscar's journey into the Catholic Church, while he was researching doctrines such as infant baptism and the Eucharist, that he had come across Ralph's website.

He was pleased to know that Oscar had listened to his videos but asked incredulously, "And you are still Catholic?" He seemed to find it unbelievable that Oscar hadn't accepted his reasoning and left the Church.

"But it was you who led me *to* the Catholic Church," Oscar told him. "I began reading the Bible and did some research—and came back into the Church."

Agitated, Ralph exclaimed, "It's not possible to read the Bible and still be a Catholic!"

Even if Ralph truly believed that, he seemed to be overreacting. Oscar told us that he began to think that surely something terrible must have happened to the man and therefore tried to respond with compassion. He quietly asked him, "Did something bad happen to you in the Catholic Church?"

Ralph dodged the question. "No smart person would be Catholic! Catholics worship a false Jesus and teach a false gospel."

The encounter continued in a similar vein for nearly an hour. Oscar dutifully explained the doctrinal foundation from sacred Scripture for the sacraments, confession, purgatory, mortal and venial sins, the Holy Eucharist, and so on. Every time, though, that Oscar supported Catholic doctrine, Ralph sneered and changed to another subject. He avoided, eluded, and ignored each of Oscar's points. He also seemed to be getting angrier and angrier. Finally, he lost his temper, shouted at the evangelists, and insulted the Rosary. Then Ralph and his assistant turned and stalked away—cursing.

Deacon Robert and Oscar said they just stood there a moment—speechless. How does one respond to such animosity? They reported that, surprisingly, they both actually felt quite calm. Neither team member can explain the peace they felt while engaged in this exchange except that it must have come from the Holy Spirit. Then Oscar remembered the quotation from Saint Peter that had come to his mind that morning and shared it with his teammate.

Thinking about it later, they said they believed that God in His Providence had prepared them for that encounter in many ways. First, during his search for the True Church, Oscar had not only listened to all of Ralph's talks but had earnestly studied each one of them. He had taken each of Ralph's accusations and misrepresentations seriously, and then had found good answers that had soundly refuted each point. In fact, as he had tried to tell Ralph, Oscar's systematic process of working through these issues had been precisely what brought Oscar back into full communion with the Catholic Church. Second, Oscar and Deacon Robert also gave credit to our Dallas SPSE social network that connects evangelists from our different teams. Each time something like this happens, we discuss the experiences thoroughly. Since I have had several encounters with professional anti-Catholics such as Ralph, Oscar and Deacon Robert were able to learn beforehand what such an encounter might be like. Third, SPSE training in general helps prepare evangelists to remain calm and loving in such situations. Finally, prayer, the sacraments, and our network of dedicated prayer warriors truly sustain us in all our efforts.

The men that Oscar and Deacon Robert encountered hated the Catholic Church. Jesus, though, has taught us to love our enemies. Our will for them is only the Good, and our prayer for Ralph and his assistant—and all those they've misled—is that each will one day rejoin the Church and end up happy in heaven with the communion of saints.

PEOPLE OF GOOD WILL

One day, a producer from Guadalupe Catholic Radio in Dallas accompanied us to observe street evangelization. Oscar and two other evangelists joined me as we set up in a park. Soon, a group of ten or twelve college students approached.

"What brings you here today?" we asked.

"We came from the State of Washington to evangelize around the campuses in Dallas," they told us. They were not Catholic. So when we offered them a Rosary, they not only declined but also seemed reluctant to spend any more time with us.

However, we continued to engage them by asking about their trip to Texas and about the different campuses they had already visited. Then they asked about what we were doing. At that point, we agreed to break into smaller groups and go sit at the nearby tables. Each Catholic evangelist went with three or four of the student evangelists. Later, Oscar reported in detail on the conversation that occurred at his table.

As they sat down, one of the young men said to him, "I have never met a Catholic on fire for Jesus. It's so nice to see it."

Oscar started discussing various teachings of the Catholic Church and gave them scriptural support for each one.

"I am surprised you know so much Scripture," another student responded. "Usually Catholics can't quote anything from the Bible."

Oscar then explained how the Bible came down to us from the first few centuries of Christianity. He described the laborious manual process that had been required to make a copy of the Bible before the printing press was invented. After a hand-crafted copy was finally completed, the precious document was then attached to the podium in the church with a chain. That way people could read it, but not be tempted to steal it.

The Rosary was the next topic. Oscar explained that the Rosary was a prayer that was also a meditation on scenes from the life of Jesus Christ and His Blessed Mother. Christians usually agree that everything that Jesus said and did has layers and layers of meaning. The beads and the prayers help people time their meditation so that they spend about five minutes thinking about a particular event—considering not only what it meant back then, but also how it applies to their own lives today.

The students became more and more receptive, and the discussion moved on to John 6 and the institution of the Holy Eucharist. Finally, the young man sitting next to Oscar said, "My roommate is going to RCIA."

"Awesome!" Oscar replied. "Why don't you go with him just to see what it's like? There's no commitment to become Catholic. You can go just to learn more about what the Catholic Church actually teaches on different doctrines."

"I might do that," he said. "I can't wait to tell him about today and meeting with a group of Catholic evangelists."

As they stood to leave, one student said, "Hey, about those Rosaries you offered earlier—I wouldn't mind having one."

Oscar's jaw dropped. "Of course! Help yourself," he said. "You can take this pamphlet, too, that explains how to say it and how to meditate on the mysteries."

After each student accepted a Rosary and pamphlet, we hugged our brothers in Christ and wished them well. What an unexpected pleasure to evangelize the evangelists! It felt so positive and uplifting to dispel once again the preconceived misconceptions that so many Christians have about the Catholic Church.

* * * * *

Each SPSE encounter is different. I hope, though, that these stories have given you the flavor of Catholic street evangelization. I have for the most part featured Oscar Cavazos here. Although Oscar's individual journey is unique, his enthusiasm for Jesus Christ and the Catholic Church is clearly evident in each of our evangelists. Just as Oscar touches the lives of many people who need what only the Catholic Church can offer, so, too, does every evangelist in our organization.

DISCOVERY

I said earlier that sending that first e-mail to SPSE was life-changing for me. Not only did new interests and new activities come into my life because of it, but changes have come to my spirit as well. Perhaps the most noticeable spiritual fruit in my own life, since beginning Catholic street evangelization, is a new experience of boldness. My wife would tell you that if you had said five years ago that I would be leading groups of people to evangelize on the streets of Dallas, she would have called the men in white coats to come take you away. Also, only a few years back, I would never have talked of religion with friends and coworkers.

Now, though, conversations just naturally seem to head that way. For example, one day recently I met an old non-Catholic friend of mine for coffee. In the past, I would have carefully avoided saying anything on the topic of faith—especially since there is such a history of animosity between his faith tradition and mine. On this day, however, the topic of salvation happened to come up during our visit. I wasn't tempted to try to change the subject or to gloss over our differences. Instead, I ended up talking in depth with him about salvation for another half an hour—and was able to dispel a lot of the misinformation about the Catholic Church that he had learned over the years.

This new boldness has also allowed me to meet at length with several different non-Catholic ministers. Again, my emphasis is on trying to clear up their misunderstandings about the Catholic Church. Once, three of us evangelists even attended a series of classes on Catholicism sponsored by a local non-Catholic church. Throughout the series, we each respectfully tried to stop some of the misinformation at its source.

In practicing Catholic street evangelization, I have also come to realize that our emphasis needs to be on what we have in common with non-Catholic Christians. This includes our mutual love for Jesus Christ, His death for us on the Cross, our understanding of the Trinity, salvation through the free gift of grace, and so on. I have also learned that evangelization is not always so much about defending the faith as it is about sharing it and showing others how their beliefs can be complemented and made whole in the Catholic Church. The gift we offer is that each person we encounter no longer has to "make do" with only the partial truths retained by his particular denomination, but he can be invited to the veritable feast awaiting him in the Catholic Church. "O the depth of the riches and wisdom and knowledge of God!" (Rom 11:33).

Chapter 9

Bloom Where You're Planted

Karl Strunk

Muskegon, Michigan

I was baptized as a tiny tot in what I am told was a Catholic church. This would seem to indicate that I am a Cradle Catholic! Yeah, not so fast. My road has been riddled with some rough spots, including some big potholes.

I grew up on a small farm in rural Michigan. To this day our village consists of less than two hundred residents. Notwithstanding the modesty of this population, we had five churches, but none were Catholic. Not a single one.

Out of convenience I attended the closest church to our house, a nondenominational covenant church. It was a simple structure with white clapboard siding and a steeple. Hard wooden pews faced a central podium with a flag on either side. We youngsters sat up front and sang songs: "Jesus Loves Me", "This Little Light of Mine", "Kumbaya, My Lord", and the like. Fifteen minutes after the service began, the six or seven of us children would be herded downstairs for Sunday school lessons. Cookies and milk awaited us; we didn't give a second thought to what the adults were doing.

I enjoyed going to our little covenant church. Donning my powder-blue suit and dress shoes with heels (it was the 70s), I carried my Bible in my hand and a couple of dollars for the collection plate in my pocket. No, my parents did not usually attend. If I had to speculate, I would say that this was how my mother and father scheduled quality alone time—not very holy of them, but effective.

That Bible, a gift from the Easter Bunny, gave me trouble. I would lie on the carpet in our kitchenette and try my darnedest to make sense of it. My mom would encourage me to read aloud while she was cooking. Although I was happy to do so, this endeavor was short-lived. As it happened, these holy pages were littered with all sorts of foreign words, like *art*, *rulest*, *thee*, *thine*, *thou*. As a result, my interest waned.

Another source of consternation in my "spiritual life" at the time was people who claimed to speak to God. Or, more accurately, claimed that God spoke to them. So many of the congregants, adult and child, would gleefully share with anyone in earshot how God had spoken to them or answered their prayers. I would pray and pray and pray, but God would never speak to me. Never. I can vividly remember one summer when I was five, running behind my dad as he embarked on some chore. Arriving at a gate separating a field from the pasture, I leaned upon the crossbar with hands clasped, closed my eyes, and fervently whispered my petition. Intrigued, my father inquired as to what I was always praying about.

"See, Dad, there is this really cool workbench at the hardware store that comes with all of these neat little tools...." As is common for any little boy, I wanted to be just like my dad.

On Christmas morning I awoke and zoomed down the stairs in my red-print footy pajamas, and there in the middle of the living room floor, all assembled and majestically adorned with tools, was that work bench. Not the plastic tools and toothless saws of today, but real tools, just miniaturized. My petitions were answered!

Throughout the next year, I spilled forth cascades of prayers, none of which seemed to produce any fruit. But what was to be made of all those people in church who claimed an interactive relationship with God? He talked to them, but not me. This was disheartening. Why was God speaking to my snotty schoolmate, who was nowhere near as good as I was? What about me? Why did God ignore me, what was wrong with me, what had I done wrong? Was I already one of those lost souls condemned to eternity in hell? Enough was enough, and I walked away from the small church community.

It wasn't long before the money my mom had given me for the offering plate (ahem, day care) was repurposed, and I would sneak off to the village store to buy candy and ice cream. Yet, every time the church came into view, I knew I was missing something. In a melancholy kind of way, I hoped the people from the congregation would miss me and invite me back, but they never did. I was drawn to return, but I did not understand why. I did not realize that in this way God really was speaking to me, tugging on my heart strings to come back.

Now, please don't think of my parents as heathens; we did go to church as a family. Yep, you guessed it, on Christmas and Easter! And on those occasions we attended a weird church in some other town. Even the windows were different, all sorts of funny-colored glass. There were pews with kneelers. (I always wondered, if the kneelers are padded, why aren't the pews?) The podium was off to the side, and in the center of the sanctuary was a giant table with no chairs. Spread out on the table cloth were a plate of food, a brass wine cup, and candles. Were the snacks going to be eaten while standing? That's not how we did it in Sunday school. Oh, and there was a cross on the wall—a cross with Jesus nailed to it. The preacher dressed funny, too. Aside from these embellishments, a church was a church, and I did not differentiate between Catholic and Protestant. As time marched on, our family began to abstain altogether from Christmas and Easter worship.

Like many fallen-away Christians, we were lured into the embrace of contemporary, secular culture. Before long, mischief took root in my own life. I inaugurated my path of misconduct by stealing cigarettes from my parents. I also stole their empty pop bottles, returned them to the store for the deposit money, and impulsively purchased meaningless wants. Fibs matured into full-blown lies, some of which were impressively creative. My mother would discipline me with a humdinger of a wooden spoon, but that was only effective for several days. As to be expected, my misbehavior escalated. I knew what I was doing was wrong, but once the pattern of delinquency morphed into a habitual routine, I was unable to find my way back.

Recognizing the perilous path that our family was on, a friend of my father, Paul, began impressing on us that we needed God in our lives. The gall of some people! And the local church just a skip and hop away from our front door would not suffice either. No, Paul relentlessly encouraged us to attend his Catholic parish. A parish? It turned out to be just like that weird church we used to visit on Christmas and Easter, only much more extravagant.

My father was already a Catholic, albeit not a very faithful one, but my mother and I knew little to nothing about Catholicism. Thus, though

I was only twelve or thirteen, we found ourselves propelled into those Wednesday evening classes, which I found mind-numbingly boring, the Rite of Christian Initiation of Adults. Paul was our sponsor. There did not seem to be a systematic approach to the classes, and information went in one ear and out the other. We were received into the Church, but, disenchanted and still confused about what was transpiring during Mass, we soon washed our hands of the whole thing and returned to what we knew, the temporal.

A DESTRUCTIVE AND TRAGIC TRAJECTORY

Within a year of dropping out of church (I cannot say "abandoning God" because I did not know God), deep trouble found its way to my door, launching my life onto a destructive and tragic trajectory.

In early adolescence I was sexually assaulted by two of my classmates. To my horror, word of the incident spread through our small community, and rumors started flying that I might be homosexual. Even my girlfriend inquired about it. Mortified, I denied the accusations, claiming the assault never happened.

Feeling like I no longer fit into a social dynamic, I began hanging out with a bad group of people, the only ones who would accept me. Or, so I thought. Concocting a false image, I began doing things of which society does not approve. Some of my so-called friends and I looted our school. I broke into two homes and committed larceny on a motor vehicle.

I reasoned that my delinquent behavior would discredit and nullify the grapevine gossip. My hope was that people would conclude that I certainly could not be homosexual if I had the guts, *machismo*, and moxie required for such aggressive and destructive acts. This sometimes worked—or else my latest misstep would at least eclipse the homosexual rumor, and all people would talk about was my being a thief or a bad apple.

I was prosecuted for those actions, and it did not go unnoticed by court officials that something was troubling me—that I was not predisposed to being delinquent—yet they did not understand what. However, I did not know they wanted to help. Yes, they informed me of their intention to help, but I thought it was a trick. Help? How? What could they do? As a result of this impasse, I was in no rush to address my problems. I foolishly kept hoping the dark cloud would simply vanish.

My parents disagreed intensely on how to handle the situation. Eventually my mom moved out. My dad loved me the only way he understood, by spoiling me with materialistic wants. He had no idea that he was feeding my fake persona.

One winter, due to abuse and neglect, my car stopped functioning. Such a scenario frightened me—in my mind, the lack of a car equated to the lack of female companionship. Having a girl on my arm was crucial to dispelling the homosexual rumor. Approaching my father about once again financing another vehicle for me turned out to be a futile attempt. Because of my desperation, we argued furiously. At his wit's end, my dad asked me to leave the house.

In my convoluted way of thinking, my world was falling to pieces around me. The next day I returned, and another argument ensued. Acting erratically and impulsively, in a fit of uncontrollable anger and fear, I killed my father. Yes, I was shocked, too. My father, my friend.

I took the life of the very person I had aspired to become. I miss him so much; all he had tried to do was to help me.

SPIRITUAL MAYHEM

That horrific event was nearly thirty years ago. I was sixteen at the time and received a sentence of life without parole. For the first eighteen years of incarceration I hated myself. If a person wanted to beat me or call me names, so what, such was deserved! I had no regard for God, either. That is, if He even existed. I mean, come on, if God truly existed, how could He have permitted me to take my father's life, to cause my mother such pain, to hurt my community? How could God have allowed me to be sexually assaulted? If God did exist, why wouldn't He bring my dad back to life when I begged for it so many times over the years, as He did Lazarus?

My spiritual life was mayhem. Even while I despised God, I felt drawn to Him in an unrecognizable way, in the sense that there was something out there bigger than I. Honorably, Paul stood at my side from the beginning. Oh, how he would labor to lead me back to the Catholic Church. No thanks, structured religion was not for me. I did, however, borrow tidbits from Buddhism, tree huggers, Judaism, pacifists, and even Christianity. Just not God! Paul could not understand this hodgepodge of religious relativism, but he did not become discouraged.

One day when writing an entry for my website, I was recalling a biblical story from Sunday school. In an effort to make sure my memory was correct, I sought to borrow a Bible from a friend. He handed me a couple of different Bibles, little and big. Huh? Surmising that it would be easier and quicker to find the desired passage in the smaller of the two holy books burning my fingers, I cracked the cover and was immediately confronted with a headache. By golly, this confounded Bible consisted of that same wretched English that dampened my spirits as a child. I was no more adept to read it now. Reaching for the doorknob to return these disappointing writings, I was overcome with an urge to open the larger Bible. Expecting to have another disheartening experience, I opened the formidable Bible to a random spot. Much to my astonishment, the words before me immediately revealed their meaning. I tried some other pages. Old Testament. New Testament. The contents made sense. Stepping back from the door, I sat on my bed and began to read. I later asked my friend what the deal was. Unbeknownst to me, there were other Bible translations besides the King James.

The work that removed the scales from my eyes was the New Living Translation. (For all of those fretting over my using a King James and New Living Translation, my preferred read is the Revised Standard Version, Catholic Edition.) My friend graciously encouraged me to hold onto his Bible for another couple of months. I didn't read it every day; after all, the contents were still alien and offered no recognizable application to this culture. And I was still absorbed in, well, myself. But increasingly, I found the writings of the apostles and prophets attractive—and in my hands more regularly. So much so, I ordered my own copy.

A MAJOR TURN

As the months passed by, it was not uncommon to observe me with my nose buried between the pages of God's Word. My roommate, a clerk for the chaplain, kept hounding me to attend a nondenominational Christian retreat called Keryx, an offshoot of Cursillo. Reluctantly, I conceded.

The Keryx folks got permission from the prison administration to conduct a four-day retreat on the prison campus. Yes, I had agreed to attend, but awash with biases I was shaking in my boots. Please excuse my crassness, but I was not looking forward to being among a bunch of pompous Bible thumpers who were undoubtedly superficial. On the first day, we passed through the doors of the auditorium where scores of volunteers had lined up to greet all of us candidates. They were singing, hugging, and claiming that they loved us. Ugh! The second day was a repackaging of the first. The whole show was a cacophony of unbearable gobbledygook to which I could not relate. However, the retreat took a turn, a major turn.

On the third evening, I was sitting in the front row listening to a minister read from the Bible and advance his reflections, when a choir of more than sixty people entered from a side door and serenaded us. Smack dab in front of me, literally within reach. These beautiful women and men were angelic. As they sang, a dark weight lifted from my heart, and I was filled with something much more real and lively, almost tangible. That's right, the Holy Spirit. I had met God. Finally! Hallelujah! I was a sopping mess of tears. Retreat volunteers rushed to comfort me. The angels before me were likewise touched with emotion, which only heightened my meltdown.

For the first time in my life, I recognized Christian love. By the end of the retreat, I was on fire for Jesus and desperately wanted and needed to be a part of this crusade. In order to do so, however, there were some requirements. Of course there were—everything good has a price of admission! It was obligatory that we attend their weekly fellowship meeting as well as participate in a Christian religious service of any tradition, a session of worship, or a Bible study. Aargh! The stodginess and perceived disingenuousness of regimented churchgoing and Bible study made me shudder. This strong adversity stems from a previous experience, of which, it is now necessary to relate. For whatever reason, on the Easter prior to this retreat, I attended Mass. It was probably our Lord working on me, but on the surface, I suspected it was for nostalgic purposes; I was grappling with grief and ached to reconnect with my past, remembering the togetherness of family.

Well, let me tell you, Easter Mass was not a good experience for me. The Catholic fellowship opened by praying the Rosary. Mind you, I had (still do) a very nice Rosary given to me by my mother, but this string of beads was little more than a sentimental reminder of her love. Other than thumbing the crucifix when feeling blue, I never learned how to pray it. Listening to them recite the same words over and over and over, I had no desire. Blah, blah, blah. And Rosaries are for old ladies. When the liturgy began, much to my surprise, most of the prayers from my youth were still familiar. But something was very different now. As a boy I recited formulated prayers because that's what I was taught, as is true for most kids. However, as an adult with a more functioning mind, I found the prayers antiquated, not in step with culture. The whole experience gave me a vibe of cultishness. I kept envisioning Hansel and Gretel being dragged in with hands and feet bound; all they were missing were the witch and a boiling cauldron! When the Mass concluded, I irreverently shared my thoughts with Deacon Roger and vowed never to return.

So now I found myself with the burden of selecting a religious service to meet the conditions of the retreat mission. By coincidence, or divine intervention, the only vacancy that fit my schedule was, of all things, Catholic Bible study! Begrudgingly, I signed up. When I entered the classroom, lo and behold, Deacon Roger was standing right at the podium. One would think that I would have shrunk up into a ball of humiliation. Nope. After introducing myself, I shamelessly informed everyone that I was only attending their group to fulfill a requirement and could not give a hoot what they were going to study. I plopped my derriere in a seat and did nothing. Impressive, eh? Beneath this uncouth bravado was a soul who wanted to participate, but was crippled by fear.

RETURN TO ROME

Challenges arose as I stumbled through the Bible throughout the ensuing year. Since I was there anyway, it was only practical to pose my queries in the Bible study. Yes, I am an opportunist! To each question, whether I engaged the fellas individually or as a group, their responses agreed with one another. Moreover, they would support their answers with Holy Scripture and history. This was puzzling to me because when I would present the same questions to non-Catholics, more often than not, their responses would clash. Gears in my brain began to engage. Something else was profoundly different, too. These Catholics did not try to force doctrine or theology; they were gentle and accommodating. Many of the non-Catholic Christians I encountered would bombard me with catchy passages from God's Word and admonish me to do this, don't do that, or ... you get the gist. This was a very topsy-turvy time during my formation. Overwhelmed by the pressure of indecision, I nearly threw in the towel.

Maturing in faith, I began recognizing Bible texts that lined up with those ceremonial prayers I had found so distasteful, which have permeated the Mass for umpteen centuries. Even the repetitious "Hail, Mary, full of grace" (cf. Lk 1:28) was in there. Swaths of the liturgy itself began revealing itself in the pages of my Bible. Also, the sacrament of reconciliation. The sanctity of marriage. Peter and the papacy. And ... well, you know. Could the Catholic Church possibly be the one True Church? Evidence was mounting, and I could fight it no longer. It was time for me to enter into full communion with the Church Jesus Christ Himself established.

Sure, I had been baptized, gone through RCIA, and been confirmed a Catholic as a young teenager, but I was now acutely aware of my poor formation and the sorry state of my soul. It would have been sacrilegious to saunter in and take Jesus in hand without grasping the implications ... not to mention my need for confession. First things first. Deacon Roger and the fellowship worked tirelessly until I was prepared to receive the sacrament of confession, the precursor to receiving the precious Body and Blood of our Lord. Whoa, I had a long list and was tormented by misgivings; surely, Father Joseph would run away in terror. He didn't. Instead, he overflowed with compassion, the perfect example of Christ. I felt washed. The ugliness from my past dissolved away. Sure, there were residuals, which I continue to deal with, but I was forgiven. Truly forgiven. Although I did not know what was happening at the time, I actually felt the sacramental blessings and graces saturate me. Euphoric. On a humorous side note, while I was sitting face-to-face with the confessor, off in the distance a band was rehearsing, of all songs, "Stairway to Heaven" by Led Zeppelin. How appropriate!

When Easter arrived, I was ready. We filled the chapel with plants scrounged from every nook and cranny. Father Joseph and Deacon Roger were present, accompanied by three visitors from the parish, and of course the Catholic prison fellowship was in attendance. You could practically smell the reverence in the air. My Catholic brothers and sister spiritually held me up while I offered myself to God. In turn our Lord filled me with His Son. I cradled Jesus in my hands, then humbly placing our Lord on my tongue, I let the tears flow. I knew my dad was present in spirit.

Now in full communion with God and the Church, I knew my formation had not ended. To the contrary, it had barely begun! Due to the restrictions in this environment, finding solid Catholic texts can be an exercise in futility. So, imagine my surprise when someone handed me a torn and tattered work concerning the Rosary. Yikes, isn't Marian devotion the antithesis to a true relationship with Christ? Jesus was enough to contend with; adding the rote words and phrases of the Rosary would only further retard my progress. Yet, despite these objections rattling around in my head, the book kept calling me. It was like a freshly hatched chick cheeping to be caressed. With great apprehension, I swallowed hard and read the book. The contents were not what I had expected. Not at all. Blessed Mary is not petitioned like some god or gatekeeper. No, instead, we ask her to intercede on our behalf with her Son, Jesus. Just like when we ask a friend or pastor to pray for us. It kind of made sense, in an unsettling way. Grabbing my Rosary, hiccupping through the formulated prayers and mysteries, I found Mary holding my hand as I approached our Lord. This acceptance did not happen overnight. After many attempts and several months, I finally wrapped my arms around our Holy Mother. Now, she is my sweet friend! And here's a consolation: praying the Rosary every day, I am in union with millions of others doing the same thing around the world, literally millions!

Prayer books and devotionals do not serve me well. The initial couple of weeks will flourish with romance, but then interest plummets. For a couple of additional days I will trudge on out of a sense of guilt, but then resentment settles in. It seems that it's just best for me to avoid spiritual aids altogether. However, a friend managed to cajole me into praying the Liturgy of the Hours, or Divine Office. Huh? As I came to find out, it is a huge body of liturgical prayer that is chanted or recited throughout the day. Intimidating, to say the least. To appease his annoying zeal, I borrowed a much less involved version, and to my bewilderment, this type of devotion was enticing and proved to be a good fit. It is time-consuming and a sacrifice, but the satisfaction outweighs any impediment. The Divine Office possesses this uncanny capacity to improve my spiritual awareness and, in a strange way, my confidence. Observing the fruits deriving from this practice, my mom expressed her unwavering love and encouragement by giving me a copy of the Divine Office. Because of her compassion, this is doubly special.

Complementing the discipline of the Divine Office, the next detour on my journey is one that—goodness, everything else has been unexpected, why should this stage be any different? I am currently in formation to become an oblate of Saint Benedict! Think of it as a third order. The Rule of Saint Benedict, albeit challenging, has been a tremendous resource in keeping my focus on Jesus. Its balance of prayer and work enhances how my religious life is being shaped. It was during the discernment process of this life choice that I came to terms with my relationship with God: He is in control, stop fighting, enjoy the ride.

By the hand of the Almighty, I was accepted into an entry-level seminary. Yes, in prison. We have a faith-based dormitory, which offers two pilot programs. One of the courses happens to be a four-year seminary program. Much to my chagrin, it is non-Catholic in content. Very non-Catholic. As can be imagined, there are times when our differing beliefs result in cold shoulders. Thus, life can sometimes be lonely. However, I have learned a great deal about our partially enlightened brothers. And I have gained much insight into myself. For instance, their zeal and moxie shamed me into digging up answers as to why I believe what I do. A benefit of this voracious determination to uncover the truth has led to a fuller formation in the Catholic faith in my own life.

KNOCKED OFF MY HORSE BY ST. PAUL

Since solid Catholic texts are difficult to come by in this environment, the Eternal Word Television Network quickly became a huge source of sustenance and inspiration to me. One evening, a weekly program, *Life on the Rock*, was featuring a grassroots apostolate called St. Paul Street Evangelization. What caught my attention was the organization's efforts to instruct individuals and groups on how effectively to make disciples of all nations. I had been a victim of know-it-alls who employ the tactic of knocking poor souls over the head with a Bible. Without doubt their intentions were well meaning, but such unbridled enthusiasm can prove to be downright obnoxious and counterproductive. I was open to an alternative. St. Paul Street Evangelization was marching to a different beat. First, SPSE advocates a nonintrusive approach. After a friendly initial overture, the evangelist waits for the person to reciprocate, never forcing a conversation on anyone. Second, instead of hammering a person with Scripture passages, SPSE evangelists simply share three minutes of how Jesus has impacted their lives. No theology or doctrine. No forceful proselytizing or religion-bashing. Not even Bible gymnastics or catechetics. If the listener is motivated to inquire further, by all means, feed him. But don't chase; let people's curiosity about your spirituality and application to life draw them. After all, it is the Holy Spirit awakening them, not us. I appreciate that this model opens evangelization to everyone, not merely the scholarly or self-anointed prophets. What an incredibly novel proposition.

Not really anticipating a response (hey, I understand the bias against people who are incarcerated), I contacted St. Paul Street Evangelization. Their curiosity must have been equally piqued because they responded with training materials! Impressed by their gentle seed-planting philosophy, I began applying it. Oh, if only it were so simple; this is where I must admit to a disaster. The first couple of chances to employ this model and share my Jesus story went smoothly. However, soon after I was consumed by pride. The next soul who expressed interest in my faith I walloped with my whole story. Well, kind of. After a half hour he fluttered off; goodness, I hadn't even gotten to the good stuff, yet! To this day the frazzled gentleman still twinges when he hears my voice! Oops.

The mission of St. Paul Street Evangelization is more than simply spreading the Word of God. There is a training component in which the ministry philosophy is passed on to others, thus expanding the breadth of their effectiveness. Having suspected that we as Catholics have become indifferent when it comes to carrying out the command of the Great Commission, I was prompted to conduct an informal survey of the guys in our Catholic fellowship. It revealed an illness, apathy. I asked the fellas, "What would you say if a person were to ask you about Jesus or why you're Catholic?" Some shrugged and said, "I don't know what I would tell them. I just am." Others said they would quote chapter and verse to the poor soul. Worse, some admitted that they would hand a person a Bible and walk away. Ouch! Without revealing how the Living Word has impacted one's life, scriptural accounts can be meaningless to someone who has no belief or foundation from which to build.

When the atmosphere is conducive, I share the techniques of SPSE with members of the Catholic fellowship. The goal is to get the fellas to become comfortable with revealing their Jesus story when approached about their Christian faith, to relax and become transparent, letting their love shine. It is inspiring to watch as they recognize that they can rely on their own relationships as a contributing resource to leading others to the Kingdom of God. It's a special moment, for sure. Ultimately, we must be better prepared to evangelize competently. Some are eager. Of course, others are happy to remain unnoticed except when it is time to be seen attending Mass.

SUDDENLY, RESOURCES

In the midst of all of this, unbeknownst to me, St. Paul Street Evangelization posted my initial inquiry on their website. That's not all. Those sneaky disciple-making missionaries attached with my letter a plea to all their evangelists to send me sound Catholic formation and study materials. Oh, goodness, the community of St. Paul Street Evangelization responded with an incredible outpouring of love. Books began arriving from all over the country. Initially I did not know what was happening. I knew absolutely none of these aspiring saints. All I could do was scratch my head in puzzlement. To show you how God can work, here's a little peek into His almightiness: all the books had one thing in common—each had the same wrong shipping address. Yet, every text was received! It was through this mailing hiccup that I was able to connect the dots. Once the picture was before me, I laughed in amazement. So touching were these gestures of kindness that my eyes leaked and my heart danced. Never have I witnessed or been the recipient of so much charity from strangers.

Because of their anonymity, expressing appreciation to these selfless souls has been impossible. The assistance and guidance of their charity has profoundly enriched my Jesus journey. My only response can be prayer and a pledge to apply these tools.

In the area of apologetics, these resources have filled me with the confidence to defend our faith. My modus operandi up to this point had been to tuck tail and scurry away when questions amounted to anything of substance. Yeah, I was always on the run. Although I have not developed the capacity to retain every nuance of what I have consumed, thanks to the angels of St. Paul Street Evangelization, I have a solid foundation on which to stand. Even on those occasions when stumped by challenging theologies, I am now in a position to suspend the debate and revisit that particular topic at a later time. Whew, that's much better than limping away in mangled defeat!

Similarly, from a spiritual perspective these resources have assisted me during times of darkness and doubt. We have all had our struggles with what seems to be an absence of God when we most desperately need Him. But an additional challenge for me has been the rigors of this environment. See, sometimes our non-Catholic brothers promote rhetoric that causes me (and, I'm sure others) to question the necessity of our faith under one, holy, Catholic, and apostolic umbrella. Yet, when I rest my troubles within the pages of the early Church Fathers, the *Catechism of the Catholic Church*, writers like Dr. Scott Hahn and C. S. Lewis (an honorary Catholic, wink, wink), the *Spiritual Exercises* of Saint Ignatius, and so on, I am rewarded with the firm hand of truth anchored securely in the Church against which Jesus promised that the gates of hell would never prevail. Brace yourselves for a strange twist. Yours truly facilitates a small Catholic study group (note, all are welcome, but the focus is on catechetics and the full canon of Holy Scripture). With the materials from SPSE, we can delve deeper into our faith. I am now able to provide a small library for any and all who wish to become more intimate with our Lord, as well as for those who desire to learn more about our doctrine and theology. Whether people are devouring or just snacking, they are being fed with the truth.

St. Paul Street Evangelization also provided a multitude of their topic-specific evangelization pamphlets, the very same ones their teams use out on the street. Knowing the "powers that be" would frown upon an impromptu information center being staged on the sidewalk or ball field, I had to be a little creative in figuring out how I would use the pamphlets in my own one-man evangelization team. Each morning I pray the Divine Office in a community room. I find a corner and turn my back to everyone while softly chanting and reciting the prayers. As much as I try to go unnoticed, people are aware of my presence. Every now and again a stray will pop by to listen. I now set a table behind me and spread an assortment of pamphlets over the top and commence to pray. Curious passersby can anonymously select a pamphlet of interest, swiftly tuck it under their arm out of sight of prying eyes, and read it at their leisure. This being a contained community, I am easily available to discuss any questions they may have. Few have inquired so far, but the opportunity is ripe. Also, due to the layout of this dorm, I periodically place pamphlets here and there on community tables. At first I was concerned that some obnoxious soul would gather and discard them, but I have monitored the outgoing trash and have seen no signs of such activity. Thus, it can be inferred that people are actually reading them ... or intend to. Remember, seeds are being planted in a non-Catholic faith dorm! Will there be a mass of converts and reverts crossing the Tiber? Probably not. But we are gently addressing misconceptions about our faith.

CATHOLIC FAITH, ONE-ON-ONE

Because of the confined nature of this environment, one easily becomes accustomed to the doings and behaviors of others. Similarly, living in a faith-based dorm, a man quickly finds out who supports his Christian ideals, who is indifferent to them, and who finds it necessary to persecute anyone with differing views.

Having observed a classmate study regularly with a group that attacks the Catholic Church as the whore of Babylon and the Pope as the Antichrist, I was full of apprehension when he approached me not long ago and shared that he had been watching EWTN. Suspicious, I mentally braced myself for some sort of anti-Catholic bigotry and gruffly responded, "Really, whatever for?" To my amazement, he went on and on about all the things he was learning. And, he was excited. Although still wary, I inquired as to whether he had any questions. Sure enough, he did: "Why do you guys pray to saints, and how can you justify confessing to priests?"

Okay, those were valid questions, and I began to take him seriously. Not wanting to rattle off a canned delivery, which could easily go in one ear and out the other, I suggested that we get together in a couple of days. So Gordon and I carved out an evening to explore his questions. I was sure to select an out-of-the-way place so he would feel comfortable and not be discouraged by peer pressure; after all, he would be seen studying with a Catholic! Also, realizing the suspicion non-Catholics have toward our complete canon, I borrowed a non-Catholic Bible to rely on when conducting this study.

Instead of beginning with Catholic reasoning per se, I first addressed the slew of Scripture verses that people often manipulate or take out of context in order to deny the truth of difficult Catholic teachings. In doing this, I sought to disarm Gordon by showing him that I was not avoiding the verses Protestants typically rely upon. This took about an hour. Ouch! I had crossed my fingers that he would not tucker out, reassuring him that we would get to the meat of his concerns. And we did.

We began using a couple of trifold pamphlets distributed by St. Paul Street Evangelization, "Praying to the Saints" and "Confession". I also pulled out the *Catechism of the Catholic Church* and a few other resources. The look on his face as the truth dawned on him in little spurts was uplifting and rewarding. After two hours I had no more oomph left. I was ready to call it a night, but he appeared poised to continue. I couldn't. I was the one who tuckered out.

However, in the ensuing months we have continued to talk and explore other questions. He's not only challenging me, but keeping me sharp. As it turns out, Gordon's family is Catholic, but he never stuck with the true faith. On coming to prison, he experimented with a variety of beliefs from Wicca to Protestantism. Like me, when he began asking questions about certain Scripture passages, he would end up with a cacophony of various responses from the Protestant fellas; however, when he spoke to me and then to his Catholic cousin on the phone, he would always get the same responses. As the questions progressed, so did his interest.

Gordon is now exploring the idea of entering the Catholic Church, and he is tackling the Rite of Christian Initiation of Adults! If I do say so with a little pride, I am his sponsor. In this process of discernment, he has not missed a single Eucharistic Service (we don't have Mass at this facility). He eloquently sums up the Liturgy of the Word as follows: "When I leave the church I can remember the Bible passages and the message which was preached!" (Okay, be patient while he learns the correct terminology.) Oh, and get this, here is a sign that the Holy Spirit is active in this conversion: he is praying the Rosary! Is that cool, or what?

* * * * *

Some of the thresholds God has invited me to cross have been easy to navigate, while others were nearly paralyzing and required much more resolve. Some crosses were heavy and bristling with fat splinters like a nasty pincushion. There were times when it seemed that God had forgotten or cast me aside. With such feelings, a person could be tempted to drop Christianity entirely, but I know this invitation of the evil one is a deceptive illusion. Not to receive Jesus in the Eucharist, to reject the generosity of the Father's forgiveness, to refuse the counsel of the Holy Spirit, to dismiss the comfort of our Blessed Mother—all these would be a catastrophic loss. Life without these graces would cease to be free.

God, thank You for Your continued patience ...

My mother deserves much credit. Through all the hills and valleys she has not given up on me. Somewhere in the ashes she perceived an ember worth saving. Her love and support mean everything. She, too, is on this spiritual journey with Jesus. It is a blessing to share this part of our lives together.

Paul, my friend and a soldier in shining armor for Christ, has been unable to witness with his physical eyes the germination and harvest of the seeds he planted because, to my sorrow, he passed away. Communion of saints? Yes! But his friendship and presence here on earth are greatly missed.

Chapter 10

Serving Others by Helping Them to Serve

Father Michael Mayer

Rochester, New York

Sam was a quiet man in his late twenties or early thirties who sat by himself at Mass. He attended only occasionally, and then would disappear for months at a time. He was often sweaty, disheveled, and sick looking. After a time, his Mass attendance became more regular, and he appeared less nervous and more groomed. He confided in our parish staff that he was battling drug addiction and had been in and out of rehab.

Then one Sunday Sam asked if he could help with the Summer Bible Camp. We weren't sure how to use his help but encouraged him to come, although we didn't really expect him to show up. But there he was early the next night. He was asked to help put up the canopies, but this turned out to be a difficult task for him. He didn't know how they worked or how to ask for help. Struggling and frustrated, he wasn't sure why he had come or what good he was doing.

However, he continued to return each night, and after a few more sessions he got the hang of it and considered erecting the canopies "his job". After the tents were up, he would just sit on the steps observing the action, then he would help clean up. On the fourth night during the cleanup, he approached Sue, one of our staff members, with a smile on his face.

"I get it! I set up the tents and the children learn about Jesus. I am part of His mission!" Sam exclaimed.

Sue was flabbergasted. She just assumed everyone understood why we do this work and how the mission of Jesus is worked out in all the little efforts we make to "love our neighbors as ourselves". Her relationship with Sam helped her to realize that a key part of Christian ministry is to help others learn what she took for granted—that all are called to be "part of His mission"—and to bring them out of themselves, helping them to serve as Jesus Christ asks. Sue realized that evangelization is as much for the everyday Catholic as it is for those involved in professional ministry, but that often people need help in reaching out to others.

INTERRUPTED VOCATION

I have been a Catholic priest for sixteen years, and spent over half of that time working in two inner-city parishes in Rochester, New York. One of them, Saint Andrew Church, is located in the 14621 zip code, one of the poorest areas in the country. Gangs, drug-dealing, poverty, and prostitution are all part of the day-to-day existence of the people in the area. The need for food is an ongoing one. Teens have told me that their parent or grandparent would lock the cupboards or refrigerator at home so that the family's food would not run out before the end of the month.

Even though I had grown up in a comfortable suburb of Rochester in the post–World War II heyday of Catholic culture in America, I was excited about a parish assignment in the inner city. Before I was a priest, during the '80s and early '90s, I had lived and worked in Washington, D.C., where I was an active member of Saint Augustine Church, referred to as the "Mother Church of African Americans in the Nation's Capital".

The twelve years I spent as a parishioner at this inner-city, black church fueled my drive to serve my underprivileged brothers and sisters. As I became better acquainted with the people around me each Sunday at Mass, I began to understand the reasonable requirements of these inner-city residents: accessible food, safe schools, affordable housing, reliable health care, steady employment, and so forth. As I grew to love the people who worshipped alongside me, I felt the desire to serve them. I got involved in various works-of-mercy programs in the parish. In particular I participated in many efforts to develop affordable housing in the District of Columbia. One of my favorite memories from my service at Saint Augustine was helping to develop a tennis program for children in the neighborhoods surrounding the parish. Also, for the last five and a half years I lived in Washington, I was employed as the program director for the National Alliance to End Homelessness. These experiences opened my eyes not only to the needs of the underprivileged but also to the reality that it is possible to make changes in people's lives through consistent, faithful action.

In the late 1990s, I sensed that God was calling me to give even more of myself, so I began to look into full-time, church-based ministry in some form. I considered the permanent diaconate, lay missionary ministry, contemplative life, and so forth, but after consulting with my spiritual director and investigating the various options, I realized that I was attracted to ordained ministry as a diocesan priest.

This surprised me because in the late '70s and early '80s, I had spent six years working with and studying for the priesthood with the Paulist Fathers. After I discerned that I should leave the community—a decision based on a wavering sense of belonging with the Paulist Fathers rather than on any crisis in faith—I thought that I would live the rest of my life as a parishioner of a parish rather than as a cleric.

I hadn't thought much about the priesthood since leaving the Paulist Fathers, but now I found that door standing open for me again. I decided to walk through it, and in 1998 was ordained a priest at Sacred Heart Cathedral in Rochester.

I realize that mine was simply an interrupted vocation, and I consider my years working and worshipping in Washington as preparation for the continuation and fulfillment of my vocation to the ordained priesthood. Indeed, those years helped give me a heart for the urban poor and a desire to serve them, a fervor that would blossom into new channels during my priestly assignments in the inner city, and yes, even in the suburbs.

THE CHURCH IN THE CITY OF ROCHESTER

After three years as an assistant priest at a large, suburban parish, in 2001 I was assigned to pastor inner-city Saint Andrew Church and a second parish that was soon closed. Shortly after this another parish was added to the mix, and the two—Saint Andrew Church and Church of the Annunciation—eventually merged to become Light of Christ Church. Since the 1960s, many white Catholics had moved out of the city and into the suburbs, so the parishes, both with extensive properties, were suffering from this exodus and were challenged by the needs of city dwellers.

Saint Andrew Church was on Portland Avenue in a depressed area known as the "Crescent". The dire poverty of the neighborhood was the fallout of gang activity, drug and alcohol abuse, unemployment, absentee landlords, and absentee parents. We did not want to be the absentee Church!

As pastor, I was privileged to have a staff who shared my drive to work in the city and to serve the needs of its residents. As our youth minister used to say when she saw the local teens congregating, "They are all my children." One staff member, before she was even hired, had not one but two cars stolen from the church parking lot. Still, this did not deter her from joining our staff. Our meetings always focused on what we could do to reach out to the people in the neighborhood, and right from the beginning of my time in the city of Rochester, our parish was community focused.

And so our evangelization efforts began. We started with an outreach program called "Faith, Food, Fun, Family, Friends and Fellowship Fairs" held on five Monday evenings on the front lawn of Saint Andrew. A glorified hot dog roast, the program drew many neighborhood children, teens, and adults. Some came to the church out of curiosity; many were drawn by the free food and became "repeat customers". The fairs were also successful in that a lot of our parishioners came to meet and serve the community. The outreach helped to unite Saint Andrew and Annunciation, which were in the process of merging, as parishioners from both churches got to know one another in the midst of service and "in the breaking of the bread".

The success of the Faith, Food, Fun, Family, Friends and Fellowship Fairs led us to reimagine our traditional Summer Bible Camp as a neighborhood outreach opportunity. Renamed "Faith First", the camp was incorporated into the already-scheduled Fairs. One canopy housed Bible stories' programs and crafts, and another hosted representatives from a variety of social agencies who displayed their information and resources. We offered horse rides, the Zoo mobile, games, bubbles, sidewalk chalk, tours of the church, and of course, hot dogs. All was free to every participant.

Our intention in developing this outreach was to move our Catholic witness from within the church building to outside it, to show our neighbors that we recognized them as our brothers and sisters and had a desire to know them, and to share with them the riches of our faith.

Parishioners happily supplied everything needed for this outreach and enjoyed serving those who came to the fairs. Indeed, it was at one of these "Faith First" fairs that our friend Sam, the "Canopy Builder", had his revelation about being part of the mission of Jesus.

We continued to develop other avenues to assist our brothers and sisters in the community. Outreach to children and teens was a particularly important part of our work in the city. When I arrived as pastor, Saint Andrew already had a Food Cupboard for the area's residents, and over the years we developed a drop-in center, a tutoring center, and an annual basketball camp that was directed by a local, professional basketball player. All these programs were free, supported by generous donations from parishioners, stores, and other organizations.

On one occasion some children who frequented our drop-in center told us that they had been evicted. We found out that they had no beds, blankets, and so forth because all they were able to take with them was their clothes. Our youth minister worked with our St. Vincent de Paul Society to provide them with what they needed. Often we would hear of the needs and problems of families through the children who came to the drop-in center and tutoring center.

Aware that we should not expect the community always to come to us, we decided to go door-to-door to better know our neighbors and their concerns. For this "Walk with Jesus"[1] we had the help of some members of a large suburban parish. We developed a survey with questions that included input about our neighbors' hopes for themselves and their neighborhood, what they would like to change, what talents or skills they had, and what particular needs they had (spiritual, food, medical care, senior care, etc.). Once we canvassed people in different parts of the parish, we collected the information and worked

[1] This is the mission statement of the "Walk with Jesus": We go out to meet our neighbors as members of St. Andrew/Annunciation/Transfiguration Catholic churches who believe in Jesus Christ, the Son of God, the Savior of the world. Through his life, death, and resurrection Christ has given us the perfect model of holy living. Our heart's desire is to be faithful and grateful stewards of this Good News of Salvation and to share it with others. We live to proclaim Jesus is Lord! With the guidance of the Holy Spirit we seek to put God first in our lives and to share the many spiritual and material blessings we have been given with our neighbors. The Holy Spirit guides and teaches us to pray, to do works of love, to speak the Word of God. The Spirit of God prepares and empowers us to serve the Lord and to invite our neighbors to join us as we draw closer to our crucified and risen Lord and Savior. We go out to our neighbors as brothers and sisters to give a blessing and to receive a blessing.

to develop and implement ministries that would serve the needs of our neighbors.

One of the most important ministries that we developed was the Beacon of Hope Clothing Boutique. For many years a scout troop or our teens would put on a one-day clothing giveaway in the basement of the school building. Once the school closed, however, our youth minister suggested setting up a permanent clothing center. With just two hundred dollars to build racks for clothing, the center was launched under the guidance of our deacon, his wife, and a religious sister who was a pastoral associate at the parish. With parish members staffing the center, the clothing boutique expanded into six classrooms. Once word got out about the center, clothing came in from churches and ecumenical groups around the county. Eventually over three hundred families were referred to us and were given the opportunity to come in four times a year to outfit their families at no cost. Likewise, anyone could stop in and buy any piece of clothing or accessory for just one dollar. Our workers sorted, mended, cleaned, and folded all donations so that only gently used items were given away. A number of neighbors who themselves had received clothing from the center eventually signed up and became volunteers.

Every year, we had a few from the surrounding neighborhood join or return to the Catholic Church, but we knew many more were touched, healed, and given hope by Jesus Himself, working through the hands of our parishioners.

My experiences in the city of Rochester showed me how important it is to focus, not only on those in the pews on Sunday morning, but on everyone living in the neighborhoods surrounding the parish. The needs of those in the city provided a catalyst for the development of outward-focused evangelization, which included not only serving the physical needs of city dwellers, but providing them with hope that only comes through the working of the Holy Spirit. Not to go out into the neighborhood and evangelize in this context would have been a denial of the most basic Christian commission.

Despite having numerous grand old churches located close to one another, many large cities have lost most of their original parishioners and their offspring long ago. Catholic parishes in the inner city, if they are to survive and flourish, need to go out to those who live around them and find out who they are and provide means of serving their physical and spiritual needs. Urban ministry must always be evangelical at its root.

THE PURPOSE OF THE CHURCH

The need to evangelize has been a recurrent theme of the Catholic Church for many years or, should I say, since its beginnings. Again and again, Catholics have been told of the need to grow in the faith, to deepen their relationship with Christ and their knowledge of the teachings of the Church, and then to go out and share their faith with others. I suspect that just about every Catholic parish has an evangelization committee, one that spends hours talking about the need for evangelization and, perhaps, develops and implements programs to provide parishioners with more information about the faith. Lenten programs, faith sharing programs, Bible study programs, and renewal events are presented with the hopes that parishioners will become more active in the transmission of their faith to their children, grandchildren, friends, and acquaintances.

However, my sense is that the evangelization of members of the Church—the "internal" component of evangelization—seldom gets translated into the "outward" component of evangelizing those outside the church walls. This may be, in part, because evangelization efforts at many parishes seem to be focused more on *information* about faith than on the individual's *relationship* with Jesus Christ. We might ask, "Do Lenten programs and Bible studies nourish our walk with the Lord, encouraging us to grow in love and gratitude for the gift of salvation from a merciful God? Or do they simply fill the need to 'learn' something about God, which is not internalized and does not impel us to share this life-giving relationship with others and invite them to enter into or deepen their own relationship with God?" I do not mean to disparage all Bible studies and Lenten programs; I simply want to suggest that most parishes and parishioners need and want more. I suspect that most parish evangelization programs are rather generic in nature and do not consciously seek to deepen members' relationship with God, but are ends in themselves.

Unfortunately, evangelization is foreign territory to many Catholics. Again and again, Catholics have said to me, "Oh, that's not for me;

I can't do that" or, "That's what Jehovah's Witnesses do, not Catholics." They find it difficult even to imagine themselves approaching an acquaintance, let alone a stranger, and starting a conversation about their relationship with God. And, yet, do we realize that the Catholic Church is what it is today because of so many faithful people going forth to preach Jesus Christ in every part of the world?

I very much value my years as a pastor in the inner city and view them as formative of my priesthood and of my understanding of Jesus' mandate to "make disciples of all nations" (Mt 28:19). Pastors are to serve their parishioners, and I have learned that a significant way of serving them is to spur and prod them to live their baptismal call to evangelize. This does not just consist of preaching inspiring homilies and writing articles for the bulletin but also of providing concrete ways for them to reach out beyond the comfortable church campus boundaries. And as a priest, I must personally model such outreach, which always includes proclaiming the Person of Jesus Christ. Just as Sue, in the story at the beginning of this chapter, realized that part of serving the Church consists of helping fellow Christians to serve others, we priests must lead our parishioners in service and evangelization of people outside our parish bounds. The outward-focused parish actively serves its surrounding community's material and spiritual needs, and at the same time bolsters the faith of its own parishioners through this evangelization.

BACK TO THE SUBURBS

After nine years in the inner city, I was reassigned to a large suburban parish, Saint Pius X, the same one where I had served my first three years as a priest. Although returning to the suburbs was somewhat of a culture shock, I welcomed the opportunity to work with suburbanites. My hope was that I could use my experiences in the inner city to help them understand the needs of the poor. I was also eager to continue reaching out to the nonparishioners living within the parish bounds and to lead my parishioners in doing the same. The fact that I was no longer in an inner-city parish did not let me off the hook for evangelization. The fact that our neighbors had their material needs met and weren't prostitutes or gang members did not mean that they didn't need to hear the good news. In fact, I knew that the rich and the comfortable can be even more susceptible to despair, depression, and dysfunction than the poor of the inner city. Everyone needs Jesus.

I was happy to see that Saint Pius X was already actively working on finding ways to reach out to both parishioners and nonparishioners alike. A vibrant program for men, a conscious effort to welcome visitors at the annual country fair, and an openness to learning from other growing parishes had helped focus the parish on finding new ways of proclaiming old truths to people both inside and outside the parish.

Then in June 2013, I was assigned to be an assistant priest at Our Lady of Peace parish in the small city of Geneva, New York. Our Lady of Peace is a typical parish in that it runs almost on autopilot, having done things in a particular way for many years. And, as in most parishes, the main focus is an internal one, on those who are members of the parish. Having been reassigned several times over the past four years, I was beginning to wonder if I would ever have the opportunity and time required to participate in an effective evangelization effort. Two things happened to encourage me to step out in faith and act.

First, a friend directed my attention to St. Paul Street Evangelization, suggesting its website was worth a look. I investigated the organization and thought that it was focused and clear and offered a simple how-to outline for evangelization. Second, David Higbee, director of St. Irenaeus Ministries in Rochester, which seeks to provide opportunities for Catholics and seekers to learn more about the Catholic faith, offered to support me in whatever programs I wanted to develop. So, I decided to offer an SPSE Basic Evangelization Training to encourage and support parishioners from around the diocese who wanted an easy and practical way of moving out of the churches and onto the streets with the gospel message.

In March 2014, Adam Janke of St. Paul Street Evangelization presented a Basic Evangelization Training to over forty people from around the Diocese of Rochester and outside it. During the two-day training, we reviewed the theology of evangelization, recent encyclicals, and current facts that emphasize the need for the Church to reengage its evangelical roots. We also learned evangelization techniques and approaches such as sharing one's personal testimony and role-played different evangelization scenarios. Attendees were very happy with the training, and it generated a good deal of discussion and energy.

STREET EVANGELIZATION

A small group of eager Catholics and I soon set up our own chapter of SPSE and began evangelizing in May 2014 at the Rochester Public Market, which thousands of people from all over the area frequent on Saturday mornings. Team members staffed an information area near the main entrance, while others wandered around the market offering people Rosaries, prayer cards, medals, prayer, and support. To date, we have evangelized at the Rochester Public Market every Saturday since that May.

I always smile at the changes people undergo between the time they first consider doing street evangelization and the first time they actually participate in an effort. People who, at first, were convinced they could never offer strangers a Rosary or medal or prayer have found the experience to be a joyful one and quickly become hooked. They are encouraged by the delight and support of fellow Catholics who see them on the street, and by the positive responses of non-Catholics and non-Christians to their offers of Rosaries and prayer.

One morning in June, a team member and I were evangelizing together at the Public Market when a gentleman approached and said that he had been watching us from a distance, very curious as to what we were up to. When we explained that we were Catholics proclaiming the good news, he was astonished and mentioned that he had never seen or heard of Catholics evangelizing in public. He told us that he was a Protestant who had done some street evangelization himself and commended us for taking our faith and Christ's charge to spread the gospel seriously—as Catholics.

Most people welcome our interactions, and some even give their own witnesses. This helps team members to see how important their presence is in facilitating and encouraging people to look at their faith and their walk with the Lord. Once, two of us were circulating throughout the Public Market handing out Rosaries, when we met a woman in a wheelchair. She was Catholic and regretted that her condition didn't allow her to go to Mass every Sunday although she did watch the Mass on television. We prayed with her, and she told us that she was thankful for her illness because it made her realize how important God was in her life. What a moving and beautiful witness of someone learning to embrace and love her cross!

And of course, we welcome the opportunity to correct charitably those who hold views contrary to Church teaching. One Saturday at the Public Market, a woman approached Karen, one of our team members.

"Good morning," the woman said. "I am collecting signatures in support of the 'Women's Equality Act'. Would you like to sign the petition?" She flashed her volunteer badge at Karen.

"What do you mean by 'women's equality'?" Karen said, although she had a pretty good idea of some of the causes the act would be championing.

"This act promotes the welfare of New York women by supporting some of the most important women's issues of today." The volunteer had rehearsed her spiel well. "The bill seeks to increase pay equity, stop sexual harassment in the workplace, end human trafficking, protect victims of domestic violence, require employers to provide reasonable accommodations for pregnancy-related conditions, and protect a woman's 'right to choose'."

"Those seem to be great causes to support," Karen said, "but that last one is where I would have to draw the line." The woman looked at Karen blankly, so Karen continued, "I am definitely concerned about women's equality; in fact, I'm concerned about the equality and rights of all people. And that includes people who are unborn. Abortion is the ultimate human rights violation because it snuffs out the life of human beings before they even have a chance to be born. Where's the equality in that? That's discrimination against someone who is the most vulnerable that a person can be."

This time the volunteer looked intently at Karen and nodded her head slowly. "You know, I never thought of it that way."

"I'm out here this morning," Karen said, "because I am a Catholic trying to tell people about Jesus and the Catholic Church. And the Catholic Church is the biggest supporter and defender of the rights of people—women, the poor, the unborn, everybody."

Although Karen did not sign her petition, the volunteer walked away with a Rosary, a guide on how to pray it, and her own little light-bulb moment concerning the real nature of abortion.

I know that our evangelists and the evangelized alike are pleased with the nonconfrontational approach that SPSE promotes. This was made clear one evening while evangelizing outside the Rochester baseball stadium, Frontier Field. We encountered several people with dour faces shouting hellfire and brimstone at passersby. Meanwhile, our group smiled, offered free Rosaries, shared the joy of Jesus, prayed with people, and said, "God bless you, have a nice evening!" A police officer who was helping to manage the heavy foot traffic made it a point to tell us what a "breath of fresh air" it was to have people sharing the gospel with joy. (I think we were having a lot more fun, too.)

GROWTH

As our St. Paul Street Evangelization chapter grows, we continue to scout out and meet at new places for evangelization: a beach, the baseball stadium in Rochester, and the farmers' market here in Geneva where my current parish is located. I am blessed to have a very active, dedicated core team of nine members. In a single week in July, we had a group evangelize at the farmers' market in Geneva on Thursday, Ontario Beach Park on Friday, and the Rochester Public Market on Saturday!

One team member also organized a door-to-door evangelization effort on behalf of her parish, which had lost many members over the years. One Saturday, five of us set out to evangelize in the suburban neighborhoods surrounding the parish. As usual, we had some wonderful encounters with faith-filled people, and, of course, had an opportunity to share our own faith. However, one thing stuck out to us. Unlike our work at the Public Market where most people are very interested in having us pray for them, a considerable number of the people we encountered while going door-to-door could think of nothing for us to pray about, but said that everything was going well. Given that the area where we evangelized was wealthy—a neighborhood of McMansions—we wondered if there might be a correlation between wealth and an unawareness of our dependency on God.

Still, that evangelization effort was not without its fruit. Late one Saturday afternoon, a man walked into the parish office of a suburban church near Rochester where the parish secretary and the Director of Religious Education were about to close up shop before the evening Mass.

"I just wanted to let you know," the man said, "that I haven't been to Mass in many years. The only reason I'm here today is because, last Saturday, two people came to my door. One of them was a priest. They gave me a Rosary and invited me to come back. Well, here I am."

"Welcome! We are so glad you came!" the DRE exclaimed.

"Thank you," the man said. "I knew I was missing something, and I think those two showed up at the right time. I just wanted to tell you all thank you." Sometimes all it takes is a simple invitation.

The Rochester SPSE team meets from time to time for fellowship and to consider different ways to develop our apostolate. One afternoon we had a picnic during which we discussed how to keep in touch with people we have evangelized and how to provide opportunities for them to learn about the faith. From those discussions flowed ideas—which we're working to develop—such as establishing "seeker" sessions, monthly gatherings at a parish where those who want to learn more about the faith can come and ask questions. To support this, while we're evangelizing, we plan to hand out cards with dates and locations of each session. We're also working to develop a "Mass mob" program to bring people from the suburbs into the city to worship at an inner-city church. And we plan to suggest to our bishop that the diocese sponsor a diocesan-wide SPSE training.

As our Rochester chapter has expanded, I am struck by the exciting and creative ideas that our members develop. To me it is a sign that the Holy Spirit is at work, generating a zeal and a joy in those who are part of this ministry. Our aim is to continue our outreach on the streets and through parishes and to invite new people to join the chapter and become evangelists.

Of course, other people participate in ways that don't involve going out on the street. Some women at a parish near ours who had formed a Rosary-making group offered to give us whatever Rosaries we needed. To date we've distributed over three thousand of these Rosaries. A group of people at our parish have also begun a Rosary-making ministry to help supply our growing need.

SEEING RESULTS

One of the first things a street evangelist learns is not to expect "results", such as on-the-spot conversions. To ward off discouragement, it is important to keep in mind the often-repeated metaphor of "planting seeds". It is always a gift from the Holy Spirit when He permits us to see that a seed has taken root. Our team found such joy and refreshment in the man who returned to Mass as a result of our door-to-door efforts.

On another occasion, a team member and I were evangelizing at the Geneva farmers' market when I noticed a man making a beeline toward us.

"Father!" he called while still several feet away. "I want to thank you."

"Hello," I said. "What are you thanking me for?"

"A few weeks ago I was here at the market, and I saw that you all were giving away Rosaries, so I took one," the man explained. "See, I'm not Catholic, but I have a Catholic friend, Pete, who had been on his deathbed for a long time. He was in a lot of pain, and I kept wondering why the Lord wasn't taking him home. I got a Rosary from you guys because somehow I felt it would help Pete on his journey home. Well, my son took the Rosary to Pete, who was then in a coma, and prayed it by his bedside, and two days later he died."

I nodded slightly, encouraging the man to continue. He smiled. "Pete was a cook who always went to the Rochester Market to get vegetables. I see it as God's hand leading me to get a Rosary for him while I was also at a farmers' market. Pete's family was so relieved when he finally passed after all the suffering he had been through. We all think my son's praying the Rosary had something to do with it. At Pete's funeral Mass, I even saw his daughter wearing that Rosary around her neck."

"Wow, it's amazing how the Lord works!" I said.

"Yes, it sure is," the man replied. "Who would have thought that I would have gotten a Rosary at a farmers' market? Well, I just wanted to thank you for being out here talking to people and praying and giving out Rosaries."

"It is our pleasure to be doing the Lord's work," I said. "Thanks for coming by to tell us your story."

As the man walked away, I smiled. That man had been evangelized. In seeking to help his friend Pete, he saw the Lord work. And now *he* was the one who was evangelizing. He couldn't help but share this story—this testimony of the Lord's action in someone's life—with other people. He had sought us out just to tell us. It was as if he couldn't contain it. I have no doubt that he will continue to share that story with coworkers, neighbors, even slight acquaintances. We were blessed with a sprouted seed in the form of evangelized-turned-evangelist. Who knows? Maybe he'll become Catholic one day....

BRINGING CHRIST TO ALL

Someone once asked me how I view the distinction and overlap between works-of-mercy outreach as people usually think of it (feeding the poor, providing affordable housing, etc.) and evangelization as such (proclaiming the good news of Jesus Christ). I see them as a package deal. Christ's interest was in the whole person, body and soul. He met people's physical needs: feeding the five thousand, restoring sight to the blind man, curing the hemorrhaging woman. And, of course, He also tended to them spiritually. He forgave sinners, convicted Zacchaeus of his dishonest ways, and called the Pharisees to task. The Eucharist is perhaps the epitome of this whole-person attitude of Christ. By His design, the utmost spiritual salve comes to us by way of physical ingestion. This is how I view evangelization—to be another Christ reaching out to meet whatever needs a person has.

As a diocesan priest, I go where my bishop sends me. Whether that's to a poor urban parish or to one in the wealthy suburbs, my mission doesn't change. It is always to bring Christ to all and to lead my parishioners in doing the same.

The Church has an obligation to proclaim the good news, that is, to do what the Church was created to do. And if proclaiming the good news is the obligation of the *Church*, it's the obligation of Catholic *people*.

I know that Catholics can evangelize. I have seen them. They can do it anywhere: at a ball field or at a farmers' market, in the wealthy suburbs or in the poor inner city, in a public area or on the doorstep of a private residence. But sometimes they just need a little guidance.

I see it as part of my vocation of pastoring souls to lead people to do what Christ calls us to do, to share His good news. And I am convinced that the Holy Spirit has so much in store for those who make that leap of faith to evangelize. God will never be outdone in generosity. He's waiting for you to give Him a little bit so he can pour a "good measure, pressed down, shaken together, running over" into your lap (Lk 6:38).

Chapter 11

We're All Heralds

Steve Dawson

Bloomington, Indiana

As of this writing, St. Paul Street Evangelization has more than two hundred teams in seven countries, and our headquarters has moved to Bloomington, Indiana. I would be remiss if I didn't provide that information in a book like this, but I hesitate to give numbers because that's not really what it's all about. Pope Francis says that "mission is not like a business transaction or investment, or even a humanitarian activity. It is not a show where we count how many people come as a result of our publicity; it is something much deeper, which escapes all measurement.... The Holy Spirit works as he wills, when he wills and where he wills; we entrust ourselves without pretending to see striking results."[1]

Lucy's doggedness in icy Idaho; Karl's creativity despite the limits of his environment; Uzi's trust in our Blessed Mother in Gangland, Chicago; Father Mike's ability to unite and rally his troops—*all* our evangelists are a testament to me of the Holy Spirit's stirring in the Church and in people's hearts, working "as he wills, when he wills and where he wills". I am continually bowled over by the responses and efforts of our evangelists "to be God's leaven in the midst of humanity."[2]

[1] Francis, *Evangelii gaudium*, The Joy of the Gospel, November 24, 2013 (Vatican City: Libreria Editrice Vaticana), no. 279.

[2] Ibid., no. 114.

The Holy Spirit has also worked on me in the past two and a half years. One of the biggest strides has been in my approach to evangelization. Consider these two conversations:

Conversation A

Steve: Hi, would you like a free Rosary?

Passerby: Uh ... okay.

Steve: Are you Catholic?

Passerby: No, I'm Baptist.

Steve: Oh, really? Did you know that the Catholic Church is the Church actually founded by Jesus Christ? See, in Matthew 16:18–19, Jesus said to Peter, "And I tell you, you are Peter, and on this rock I will build my church, and the gates of Hades shall not prevail against it. I will give you the keys of the kingdom of heaven, and whatever you bind on earth shall be bound in heaven, and whatever you loose on earth shall be loosed in heaven." By giving Peter the keys, Jesus was hearkening back to an Old Testament passage that His Jewish audience would have been aware of, Isaiah 22:22, in which the Lord God was removing the king's steward Shebna and replacing him with Eliakim. The Lord God says of the new steward Eliakim, "And I will place on his shoulder the key of the house of David; he shall open, and none shall shut; and he shall shut, and none shall open." So, you see, whoever has the keys has the authority. Jesus gave Peter the keys and so was investing authority in him as the first—Oh! Where did he go? I guess he must have been in a hurry.

Conversation B

Steve: Hi, would you like a free Rosary?

Passerby: Uh ... okay.

Steve: Are you Catholic?

Passerby: No, I'm Baptist.

Steve: That's great that you're Christian. Where do you go to church?

Passerby: Well, I don't really go anymore. I started taking two grad classes, and I'm super busy right now. I'm sure God understands, though.

Steve: Yes, I'm sure God does understand your busy life and is right there with you helping you with your studies. Let me ask you a question, do you have a girlfriend?

Passerby: Yeah, why?

Steve: What do you think your girlfriend would say if you told her you were too busy to spend time with her and couldn't even give her one hour on Sundays? Do you think she would understand?

Passerby: Hmmm ... yeah, I see your point. But still, I don't think all that church stuff is for me.

Steve: But you said you used to go to church, right?

Passerby: Well, yeah ... "used to" as in when I was a kid. I guess I don't see any relevance in church.

Steve: That's exactly how I used to be. You couldn't pay me to go to church. But then God intervened in my life in a major way. Do you believe in God?

Passerby: Yes, definitely.

Steve: Did you know that God has asked us to come to church to pray to Him on Sundays? God doesn't require this of us to be demanding and make our lives more hectic. He knows what's best for us human beings that He created and loves like crazy, and all the rules He's put in place are to help us grow and blossom into our best selves. Let me ask you this—who would you trust more to know how your lawnmower works and how to maintain it, the engineer who designed it or your neighbor who just bought one?

Passerby: The engineer.

Steve: Right. That's God. He designed us and knows how we work and how to keep us in top condition. Fifteen years ago, I never would have believed that. I thought I knew what was best for me. I did whatever I wanted and didn't give God a thought. But you know what? I was miserable. When I hit rock bottom, God intervened, and it changed everything. Now I live for Him. I know that God's always looking out for us—after all, He sent His Son,

Jesus, to earth to die on the Cross to save us from our sins. Hey, do you have a CD player? This CD is called "True Worship", and it explains how the Catholic Mass is the highest form of worship, the worship God intends all men to give to Him, not for His sake, but for theirs. I think it'll help you understand why it's important to go to church on Sundays.

Passerby: Oh, great, thanks.

Steve: Sure. When you finish listening to it, give me a call and we can talk about it. I can even take you to a Catholic Mass. Here's my card—call me anytime.

* * * * *

These conversations illustrate how my approach to evangelization has changed since the beginning of our apostolate. I used to be very apologetics driven, eager to channel every conversation into a direction where I could show from Scripture, history, or logic how the Catholic Church is right, as in Conversation A. I hoped in this way to lead people to see the truth of Catholicism and so desire to embrace it. The problem is that very few of my listeners were in a place to understand and benefit from such an explanation. A nominal Protestant who barely pays any attention to God in his life will not give a hoot about what it means for Jesus to give some figurative keys to Peter. You can almost see Mr. Passerby's eyes glaze over.

In contrast, in Conversation B, I do not launch into an apologetics soliloquy the first chance I get. Instead, I seek to find out where the Passerby is coming from spiritually. I ask questions and listen, trying to engage the other on a level where he can understand. Some of my questions do challenge the Passerby, but in a compassionate, respectful way. I also share with him some of my own testimony, to give him something to relate to and to show him that conversion is possible. I want him to think, *Wow, here is a guy who at one point couldn't be paid to go to church, and now he spends his time on the street telling others about Jesus.*

I have learned—both through study and experience—that although apologetics, or giving a reasoned defense of a particular point of faith, plays a part in evangelization, it is not the primary part. What has to happen first and more importantly is the proclamation of the Person of Jesus Christ and the salvation He offers mankind. This essential message of the gospel is called the *kerygma*,[3] from the Greek words for "proclaim" and "herald". It is only through hearing the *kerygma* proclaimed that a person can accept faith in Jesus through the action of the Holy Spirit. Pope Saint John Paul II emphasizes the essential role of proclaiming the *kerygma* in evangelization:

> In the complex reality of mission, initial proclamation has a central and irreplaceable role, since it introduces man "into the mystery of the love of God, who invites him to enter into a personal relationship with himself in Christ" and opens the way to conversion. Faith is born of preaching, and every ecclesial community draws its origin and life from the personal response of each believer to that preaching. Just as the whole economy of salvation has its center in Christ, so too all missionary activity is directed to the proclamation of his mystery.[4]

Giving one's personal testimony goes hand in hand with the proclamation of the *kerygma*. The message of salvation is strengthened and given more credibility in the eyes of the listener when he also hears how it has been concretely manifested in someone else's life.

Apologetics cannot bring a person to faith like hearing the *kerygma* can, but apologetics can be useful in removing obstacles that hinder someone from receiving the *kerygma*. Or if a faithful non-Catholic Christian already knows Jesus and is living for Him, apologetics can help that person come to understand that the Catholic Church has the fullness of the Christian faith.

[3] One formulation of the *kerygma* is as follows:

1. *God loves us.* We are made in His image and likeness and are meant for a deep, loving relationship with Him.
2. *Sin and death.* Because of sin, we have broken this friendship with God. The consequence of sin is death and eternal separation from God in hell.
3. *Good news of salvation!* The Son of God became man in Jesus Christ, died on the Cross, and rose from the dead for the forgiveness of sins and for our salvation.
4. *The Holy Spirit.* God will send us His Holy Spirit who changes us, perfects us, fulfills our every desire, and ultimately brings us to eternal beatitude in heaven.
5. *Our response.* We must respond to this good news by repenting of our sins, believing in Jesus Christ, and being baptized.
6. *The Church.* We must commit our lives to Jesus and live as disciples in His Catholic Church. The Church will be our guide and a source of God's grace in our lives.
7. *Go make disciples.* Jesus sends us to share this good news of salvation with the whole world.

[4] John Paul II, *Redemptoris missio*, On the Permanent Validity of the Church's Missionary Mandate, December 7, 1990 (Washington, D.C.: United States Catholic Conference), no. 44.

Although at the beginning of St. Paul Street Evangelization, I used a lot of apologetics perhaps inappropriately, I did sometimes share the *kerygma*, too, as in the conversation with Joey (aka, Giuseppe) in chapter 2 who came to Mass and confession with me. I also told him my own conversion story, one that he could certainly relate to. And there were times in the early ministry when apologetics was just what was needed, as in the conversation with the Protestant couple in chapter 2. The couple already had a faith life centered on Jesus, but they were confused by the conflicting teachings of the different Protestant denominations they had encountered. It was appropriate for me in this case to use Scripture and reasoning to try to help them to see the Catholic Church as the one, True Church founded by Jesus Christ.

BOUND TO EVANGELIZE

In SPSE's evangelization training, we emphasize this distinction between using apologetics and sharing the *kerygma* and the place each one has in evangelization. We want all our evangelists to understand what we have learned—that sharing the saving gospel message, the *kerygma*, is the essence of evangelization, with apologetics taking a supportive role.

Our evangelists discover that there is a bonus to the primary place of the *kerygma* in evangelization: it means that anyone can evangelize! If evangelization were all about apologetics, we would want to make sure we always had our most educated, seasoned apologists out on the streets, but Pope Francis tells us that "every Christian is a missionary to the extent that he or she has encountered the love of God in Christ Jesus."[5] It is more important for an evangelist to have a relationship with Jesus and a love for His Church than to have a theology degree or a comprehensive background in apologetics.

I am sure a lot of people breathe a sigh of relief at this fact because not only *can* every Catholic evangelize just by sharing about his relationship with Jesus, but everyone *should*! Everyone is *supposed* to do so! Pope Francis reminds us that "in virtue of their baptism, all the members of the People of God have become missionary disciples (cf. Mt 28:19). All the baptized, whatever their position in the Church or their level of instruction in the faith, are agents of evangelization."[6] So all Baptized

[5] Francis, *Evangelii gaudium*, no. 120.
[6] Ibid.

Catholics are bound to evangelize, but thank goodness that they don't need to have the knowledge of Steve Ray or Patrick Madrid!

Great, you might say, *all you need to evangelize is a real relationship with Jesus. But,* you continue with admirable candor, *what if my relationship with Jesus is nothing special? What if I don't feel that there's anything particularly exciting to share about it? Further, what if I don't* want *to tell others about it?*

Pope Francis addresses the concern of feeling or being lukewarm and of apathy toward evangelization: "The primary reason for evangelizing is the love of Jesus which we have received.... If we do not feel an intense desire to share this love, we need to pray insistently that he will once more touch our hearts. We need to implore his grace daily, asking him to open our cold hearts and shake up our lukewarm and superficial existence."[7]

Fidelity to prayer is not easy, but it's an antidote to a lukewarm relationship with Jesus and to a fear or reluctance to sharing the good news. As part of this prayer, Pope Francis encourages reading the Gospels "with the heart":

> The best incentive for sharing the Gospel comes from contemplating it with love, lingering over its pages and reading it with the heart. If we approach it in this way, its beauty will amaze and constantly excite us. But if this is to come about, we need to recover a contemplative spirit which can help us to realize ever anew that we have been entrusted with a treasure which makes us more human and helps us to lead a new life. There is nothing more precious which we can give to others.[8]

When Jesus sees us reaching toward Him with faithfulness and sincerity, begging for zeal, reading His Word, and "asking him to open our cold hearts and shake up our lukewarm and superficial existence", He will not refuse us. We must trust in His goodness and generosity—and in His timing.

LEAVING SECURITY ON THE SHORE

However, we must also remember that the life of faith is not about feelings. Not feeling motivated or passionate about evangelization is not an excuse to skip evangelizing! Prayer should be our first recourse if we feel

[7] Ibid., no. 264.
[8] Ibid.

afraid or hesitant, but the next thing to do is just to go do it! Many times we may not feel like evangelizing, but God honors our obedience and wants us to trust in Him, not our feelings.

Consider the legend of Saint Peter, fleeing Rome to escape Nero's persecution of Christians. On the road outside the city, he encountered the Risen Christ making His way into Rome. "Where are you going, Lord?" Saint Peter asked. Jesus replied, "I am going to Rome to be crucified again," and then disappeared. Saint Peter promptly turned around and returned to the city where he would later face his own crucifixion. Out of fear, Saint Peter had been fleeing his obligation to lead the Church in Rome, but after an encounter with Christ, i.e., prayer, he resolutely set out to do what he did not want to do.

For a lot of people, evangelization is not easy. Many find it intimidating and worry what others will think of them. My wife Maria was very reluctant to start evangelizing at the Saturday Market in Portland and almost didn't do it at all. Adam still gets initially nervous when he goes out on the street. Dan, one of the teens in Flint, had a fierce battle with fear the whole first day he evangelized. And Lucy had a constant worry that a sniper would gun her down at any moment!

However, as the saying goes, "Nothing ventured, nothing gained." By far, the most common report I hear from evangelists is that the reward of sharing the gospel with someone overwhelmingly beats the discomfort of that initial apprehension. And there is more, Pope Francis tells us in strong, unmistakable language: "The Gospel offers us the chance to live life on a higher plane, but with no less intensity: 'Life grows by being given away, and it weakens in isolation and comfort. Indeed, those who enjoy life most are those who leave security on the shore and become excited by the mission of communicating life to others.' When the Church summons Christians to take up the task of evangelization, she is simply pointing to the source of authentic personal fulfilment."[9]

The Pope is saying that *by telling others about Jesus, we are becoming our truest selves*! Talk about a reward! The Holy Father continues, "For 'here we discover a profound law of reality: that life is attained and matures in the measure that it is offered up in order to give life to others. This is certainly what mission means.' "[10]

[9] Ibid., no. 10.
[10] Ibid.

And who modeled that meaning of *mission* better than Jesus Himself? The humility of the Incarnation, the obscurity and poverty of His earthly life, His immolation in the Passion and Crucifixion—"unless a grain of wheat falls into the earth and dies, it remains alone; but if it dies, it bears much fruit" (Jn 12:24). And such fruit! The glory of the Resurrection and the salvation of mankind!

Evangelization can be difficult, but Christians shouldn't shy away from hardship. We know the cross is part of our calling. Like the grain of wheat, the person who "falls into the earth and dies" by giving himself sincerely to the challenge of sharing the gospel with others also "bears much fruit." As we've seen, this fruit is not necessarily on-the-spot conversions, but it is always fruit in the evangelist himself, who in bringing the good news of salvation to others is embracing "the source of authentic personal fulfillment"!

So let us "leave security on the shore and become excited by the mission of communicating life to others"! Let us allow the Holy Spirit to work in and through us, attracting souls to the beauty of Christ. On the street, in our homes, in the workplace, across the fence, let us not be afraid to speak the truth in love (cf. Eph 4:15). "Woe to me if I do not preach the gospel!" (1 Cor 9:16) says Saint Paul, and all Christians should echo his declaration.

ACKNOWLEDGMENTS

In most cases, and certainly in mine, writing a book is not a one-man task. I sincerely thank the evangelists whose stories we've featured, for their willingness to share about their lives and experiences, and for the time and effort they've given to the formation of this book. Thank you, Oscar Cavazos, Ed Graveline, Adam Janke, Paul Mathers, Rev. Michael Mayer, Uzi Mendez, Lucy Stamm, Karl Strunk, and the teens who evangelized at the 2013 and 2014 Flint Mission Project.

I also acknowledge all the people whose behind-the-scenes work and expertise were indispensable to this project: from interviewing and drafting, to editing and revising, to advising and praying, to babysitting so others could work and supporting in untold other ways. Thank you, Carole Breslin, Celia Dawson, Maria Dawson, Maximilian Dawson, Nicholas El-Hajj, Rev. Charles Fox, Peter Herbeck, Mark Hornbacher, Katelynn Kiefer, Dave Mahoney, John Martignoni, Ralph Martin, Dianne Michalik, Marcia Michalik, Clare Newman, Gina Patchell, Grace Podges, Steve Ray, Beth Schuele, Lucy Stamm, Bernadette St. Andrew, Claudia Taniguchi, Archbishop Allen Vigneron, and Ellen Willson.

Well after the founding of St. Paul Street Evangelization, I learned that other Catholic organizations that publicly evangelize do exist. I acknowledge these, and especially the ones I know of, the Catholic Evidence Guild and the Legion of Mary, for taking our gospel mandate seriously.

Above all, I thank and honor the Holy Trinity and Our Lady of Guadalupe, Star of the New Evangelization, for their constant guidance, protection, inspiration, and grace.

GET INVOLVED

For more information about St. Paul Street Evangelization or to get involved, please visit streetevangelization.com.